# PERSPECTIVES ON GERMAN REALIST WRITING

## Eight Essays

Edited by

Mark G. Ward

The Edwin Mellen Press
Lewiston/Queenston/Lampeter

**Library of Congress Cataloging-in-Publication Data**

Perspectives on German realist writing : eight essays / edited by Mark
G. Ward.
    p.    cm.
    Papers presented at a symposium held in Nov. 1992 in Glasgow,
Scotland.
    Includes bibliographical references and index.
    ISBN 0-7734-9022-1        ) 00045978
    1. German fiction--19th century--History and criticism-
-Congresses.  2. Realism in literature--Congresses.  I. Ward, M. G.
(Mark G.)
PT763.P47  1994
833'.70912--dc20
                        94-12815
                           CIP

A CIP catalog record for this book is available from the British Library.

The Edwin Mellen Press                 The Edwin Mellen Press
Box 450                               Box 67
Lewiston, New York               Queenston, Ontario
USA 14092-0450                 CANADA L0S 1L0

The Edwin Mellen Press, Ltd.
Lampeter, Dyfed, Wales
UNITED KINGDOM SA48 7DY

Printed in the United States of America

*"Realismus ist nicht, wie die wirklichen Dinge sind, sondern, wie die Dinge wirklich sind."*

Bertolt Brecht

# Contents

# Preface

On the afternoon and early evening of Friday, 20 November 1992, a number of academics from universities in Great Britain began to converge on Glasgow, by rail, car and 'plane. The purpose was in one sense quite modest: to meet quietly in pleasant surroundings in Tarbet on the side of Loch Lomond, and to spend some two days talking about and discussing German literature of the mid- to late-nineteenth century, specifically the literature which is normally accounted realist or which represents the contribution of the German speaking world to the realist enterprise of the nineteenth century European tradition. The idea for the meeting had been formulated some twelve months earlier and had been deliberately couched in as general and open terms as possible. The focus was to be provided simply by the topic with no thematic, stylistic or any other manner of conceptual prescription other than a concentration on the prose medium. Participants were left to set their own area of investigation and within that loose structure it was largely a question of 'wait and see': the serendipity principle was to have the upper hand.

In the event, the forty eight hours that were spent in that climate of variety, ranging from bright sunshine to snowfalls romantically illuminated by the lights of the hotel, produced a meeting of quite remarkable intellectual cohesion. The common concern which emerged both in the papers delivered, and in the discussion arising from and surrounding those papers, was informed by a belief that the widespread judgement that German realist writing in some way falls short of the major literary achievements of other European cultures urgently required a corrective and some redress. As Martin Swales puts it in his contribution, the premise that 'German prose literature has often been held to be pretty marginal - or, indeed, marginally pretty' when measured in the scales of the major achievements of the social realist novel, set the backdrop for the approaches which the individual participants elaborated in their contributions.

That which unites the approaches, some of which take theoretical considerations as their starting point and some of which aim to broaden the often very narrow text base from which discussions of German Realism proceed, is the perceived need to move beyond the confines of the traditional parameters of criticism and scholarship. There is a shared belief implicit in all of the contributions that the constricting circle of academic discourse that has held sway in discussion of this literature has run out of energy and no longer contains the potential for initiating new lines of enquiry. For that reason David Jackson's opening survey of the tradition of scholarship is a timely reminder of the constraints, perhaps necessary, perhaps inevitable and certainly historically conditioned, which criticism has imposed on itself and by virtue of which key dimensions of the Realists' experience have had to remain unspoken in critical debate.

The contributions all betray the awareness that German Realist writing cannot be accommodated within models of Realism, however sophisticated, which are premised on the principle, even criterion, of correspondance. While fully acknowledging the idea of the German 'Sonderweg' and hence inevitable differences in the German tradition in any mimetic undertaking of the re-presentation of extra-literary reality within the literary text, the papers are very alive to the possibility of other manners of possible connection between the stuff of fiction and the socio-historically specific world in which that fiction was produced and consumed. 'L'effet de réel' is not, and need not be, a function of the transcription of known historical fact and data into the literary text; Keller's Seldwyla may have remained unchanged for three hundred years, it may still lie in a setting deliberately divorced from the channels of nineteenth-century economic activity, and Keller may even, over and beyond that, refuse the possibility of typicality, opting instead to concentrate on 'einige sonderbare Abfällsel', but none of that precludes a demonstration of different modes within which the historical world can imprint itself on the textual.

Central to this reorientation away from mimesis is the widely shared understanding that referentiality within the ambit of unproblematised empiricism is no longer an unquestioned or unquestionable, (even desirable) criterion in establishing the presence, or status, of Realism. Whatever the degree of subscription to, or rejection of, much of what has happened in the debate on cultural and literary theory since the early 1960s, simple notions of the autonomy of texts and authors, of the transparent and objective nature of language and its capacity neutrally to open a window onto another world in an act of documentation and recording, are no longer viable conceptual tools. However much the surface illusion the literary text creates may seem to be an undistorting reflection of an extra-textual reality, it is itself an illusion. That the text occupies a conditioned cultural space and that its identity, meaning and significance are generated within systems whose limitations it must acknowledge, perhaps at the same time as revising and overcoming them, are lessons that have fed, sometimes directly, sometimes more obliquely, into this collection of papers.

One central point of orientation that emerges stems back to 1988 and the publication in the *Modern Language Review* of an article by Martin Swales entitled "'Neglecting the Weight of the Elephant ...': German Prose Fiction and European Realism'. The central thesis argued here, of a dialectic between imagination and social constraint, of autonomy and determinism, of the reciprocal conditioning of individual feeling and thought on the one hand, and corporate structuration on the other, weaves its way as a leitmotif of conceptual focus through many of the papers. Crucially this provides a criterion for approaching the status of German Realism which bypasses, not in neglect but in argued rejection, the presumption of overt referentiality as a necessary precondition for status as realist fiction, and which then opens a path to consideration of texts as semiotic constructs, as literary workings of experience, which derive their value from their constitution as a reflective medium, where their reflective capacity is dissociated from an understanding of mimetic function as traditionally conceived. Indeed reflectivity is seen to become reflectivity *on*, and the focus of the *on* is not the static social world of things and objects, but rather a dynamic world of process, where process can be the accommodations and representations of the mental life of characters, the ebb and flow of the matrix of relations as a text finds its place amongst its intertexts, or even the very process whereby the literary texts presume to establish a determinate range of meaning.

What all of this indicates is a high degree of self-consciousness and self-awareness on the part of the writers discussed. Whether it be on the level of character portrayal, or of the adoption and adaptation of narrative structures and codes, or of the manipulation of symbol and motif, or of the attempts to yield through the evocation of localised or historical worlds a sense of the experience the German-speaking area in the nineteenth century, throughout the writers are shown to be very alive to the problems posed by their position in a world of rapid change. For all the truth that may sustain the notion of the German 'Sonderweg' and the concomitant presumptions of economic, social and political backwardness, the experience of transition, the knowledge of the loss of a previous era of (mythical?) certainty and with that the opening vistas of an uncertain future have crucially conditioned a sustaining sense of provisionality and relativity. It is this latter sense which occasions the many tensions to which these papers draw attention: tensions between autonomy and freedom in the areas of morality and motivation; tensions between the confines and dictates of inherited narrative forms and structures and the necessity of redefining, even subverting and dismantling these, in order to achieve a viable mode to speak to the contemporary world; tensions between ideological positions whose formulation is riddled with the contradictions of nascent thought, not yet formulated and theorised, but felt as the necessary response to the emergence of a new world whose future shape may be clouded in uncertainty but which is emphatically different from what had gone before.

While all this may seem to suggest a kind of uniformity of preoccupation in the following papers, there are nevertheless quite properly differences in focus, emphasis, and theoretical positions. For some the degree of materialist determination to which realist writers would seem to subscribe is all pervasive - thus the contributions on 'Self-Reflexivity', 'Stifter's *Bunte Steine*' and 'Ida Hahn-Hahn's *Gräfin Faustine*' follow through the idea of the corporate structuration of individual mentality with a fair measure of consequentiality, while others such as 'Poetic (symbolic) Realism' and 'Realism and Moral Design' are perhaps more dialectical in approach, preserving levels of consciousness in both authors and characters, which for all their cruel limitation, nevertheless bespeak a degree of autonomy and freedom. Crucially, however, there is underlying agreement concerning the area which should properly constitute the focus of debate and crucially this is all sustained by the recognition of a degree of sophistication in German realism which stretches far beyond the oft-acknowledged stylistic finesse of that literature. Above all there runs through the following papers a vibrant conviction that the Cinderella area of German Realism does have a contribution to make, that is is not a backwater, and that its choice of subject matter, so often an obstacle to its recognition particularly within a

European context, is at most of marginal relevance to its true status.

I should like to take this opportunity to thank my colleagues for their efforts in putting together this volume, that is for agreeing in the first place to attend the symposium and for subsequently providing their papers for publication. As I observed at the beginning of this Preface, the forum was informal and hence the tone of many of the contributions both reflects and sustains that informality. The whole enterprise was exploratory in nature and it is then entirely appropriate that the papers should convey that sense of quest and, on occasion, even mission.

Mark G Ward
Glasgow, December 1993.

# The 'Strengths' and 'Weaknesses' of German Poetic Realism

by David A. Jackson

The supposed 'strengths' and 'weaknesses' of German Poetic Realism have, like the entity itself, been constructed in the course of a long process. We cannot stand outside or above this continuum and pretend to be absolute aesthetic arbiters. In the first part of this paper I want therefore to review this developing tradition in order to show how very real, ideological considerations shaped definitions of strength and weakness. Then I shall go on to suggest some of the strengths and concomitant weaknesses which it became difficult to recognise in Poetic-Realist writers once the critical debate was confined within certain parameters.

A striking feature of even recent books and articles on German Poetic Realism is the extent to which, despite the new terminology, so many of their focusses and value judgements in fact echo pronouncements which predate anything one terms Poetic Realism. Even before it had even been conceived, Poetic Realism was doomed to be a second-class citizen. Why?

By the 1830s the view was widely held that, with the Art Period finally over, German literature could only flourish afresh once the provincial backward German states had achieved the benefits of national unity, freedom and a vibrant capitalist economy already enjoyed by France and Britain. Works of art written in the interim would, it was claimed, inevitably be derivative, minor, provincial. [1] A seductive notion, which has persisted down to the present, gained credence, namely that literature of the highest order cannot be produced without national unity, representative institutions, a capital city for advanced, metropolitan intellects, a buoyant capitalist economy and the resultant socio-economic movement. These correlates may flatter Anglo-Saxon prejudices; but they remain for all that a shaky construct.

After the revolutionary solution failed in 1848, publicists and writers like Julian Schmidt and Gustav Freytag adapted this historico-cultural scenario to a Borussian, *kleindeutsch* perspective revolving round middle-class ethical excellence and capitalist enterprise.[2] Instead of bemoaning the backwardness of the German states and the present inappositeness of literature, they elaborated a vital socio-political role for an 'ideal' or 'true' realism. Writers were to evoke underlying potential rather than concentrate on apparent surface blemishes. Old aesthetic distinctions between common, actual reality and ideal, true reality were clearly highly congenial to these critics. This understanding of realism also enabled liberals who had laid the blame for the 'excesses' of 1848 at the door of radical Vormärz writers, to distinguish this German version of realism from French and English ones which, so they alleged, undermined morality and painted an unfavourable picture of the middle-classes, the family and capitalism. Reading many later critics, one could be forgiven for thinking that Schmidt's and Freytag's prescriptions were in fact followed by the so-called Poetic Realists, that they did commend the middle-classes, did confine themselves to gentle humour, and did avoid biting irony, satire, caricature, etc. Poetic-Realist writers did tend to agree with Schmidt and Freytag about the need to avoid the formlessness of the English novel and the 'objective', 'impersonal' 'impassivity' of Flaubert. However - and this has to be emphasised - while the theorists of the 1850s and early 1860s may have allotted literature a socially useful role, they still believed that during this transitional period authors could produce only a literature of anticipation. The age

---

[1] See, for example, G. G. Gervinus, *Geschichte der poetischen National-literatur*, (Leipzig, 1835 - 42).

[2] Useful material on the champions of Poetic Realism in the 1850s and 1860s is contained in: H. Widhammer, *Realismus und klassizistische Tradition. Zur Theorie der Literatur in Deutschland 1848-1860*, (Tübingen, 1972), and idem, *Die Literaturtheorien des deutschen Realismus (1848-1860)*, (Stuttgart, 1977); H. Kinder, *Poesie als Synthese. Ausbreitung eines deutschen Realismus-Verständnisses in der Mitte des 19. Jahrhunderts*, (Frankfurt am Main, 1973); U. Eisele, *Realismus und Ideologie. Zur Kritik der literarischen Theorie nach 1848 am Beispiel des 'Deutschen Museums'*, (Stuttgart, 1976).

of true literary greatness still lay ahead.

When national unity was at last achieved in 1870/71, publicists and professors applied themselves with gusto to standardising and simplifying the German past. German literature and culture had to be shown to be the product of a necessary, world-historical process. Regional diversity, competing trends and traditions were disparaged, distorted, ignored. The gap between the real and the ideal seemed about to disappear for ever. Mimetic, realist fiction would now, it was believed, be at the same time classical, monumental, and heroic. Pre-1870 Poetic-Realist literature became largely redundant.

In the 1880s Erich Schmidt articulated the by then standard contrast between dynamic Imperial Germany and its predecessor, a supposedly idyllic, provincial, fragmented land of burghers, thinkers and unworldly poets.[3] Now one could afford to adopt a more positive tone towards the pre-Imperial past. At the same time, however, in order to become *die gute alte Zeit*, it had to be depoliticised, turned into a quaint, cosy idyll. Poetic Realism had to be divorced from Young Germany and radical trends in the Vormärz. This Wilhelminian amalgam of feelings - superiority, condescension and nostalgic affection - would persist in critical judgements for decades to come. It destroyed any hope of appreciating the critical, socio-political component of Poetic Realism. The naturalists for their part largely dismissed the Poetic Realists, reiterating the charge that they were minor figures producing genre pictures and petty, miniature art.

As the rivalry with France and Britain intensified, so too did the emphasis on Germany's superior cultural identity. This alleged separateness complemented Germany's supposed political *Sonderweg* . As the 1870 caesura faded, the qualities formerly attributed to pre-1870 Poetic-Realist works were now both extended forward beyond 1870 to writers' later works and also revalued upwards: they were praised as incarnating the distinctive strengths of a unique German cultural tradition. Thomas Mann's work *Betrachtungen eines Unpolitischen* (1918) is typical of this view. Mann reiterated the claim that the German Poetic Realists had not been interested in politics in the western-liberal/democratic sense or in commenting on social or class issues; that radical, democratic views were alien to them; that they had set no store by the critical intellect or the 'western' progressive-humanitarian tradition dating from the Enlightenment. Instead he commended as their strengths an alternative slate: spirit, soul, *Gemüt* , imagination, feeling, *Stimmung, Humor, Innerlichkeit, Bürgerlichkeit, Heimat-*

---

[3] See E. Schmidt, *Charakteristiken I*, (Berlin, 1886).

*gefühl, Nation,* etc. While Mann's general ideological position during this period has long since been subjected to close critical scrutiny, the criteria elaborated here still often underpin many statements about Poetic Realism.

During the Weimar Republic the focus did not really change. The academic establishment was firmly conservative; outsiders like Georg Lukács could not break the consensus about the German, anti-Enlightenment character of Poetic Realism. The distortions of the Nazi period need not detain us here. On the other hand, the situation after 1945 crucially shaped critical attitudes down to the present. In retrospect it is easy to see why after 1945, particularly among German-Jewish refugees like Erich Auerbach, the supposed strengths of Poetic Realism were suddenly transformed into weaknesses.[4] In the debate about the relative merits of two allegedly distinct cultures the scales now tilted overwhelmingly in favour of the west. Backward in political, social and economic terms, nineteenth-century Germany could only produce works which reflected this sorry state. As we have seen, publicists were saying the same thing in the 1830s. The works of the Poetic Realists supposedly lacked both western realism's affirmation of liberal-humanitarian values and any sense of history in the making. Because of its undoubted stature, Auerbach's book made a great impact. German Poetic Realism seemed trapped for ever in a separate, inferior sphere, divorced from the mainstream of liberal-democratic culture.

Faced by such wholesale questioning of the German cultural tradition and desperately needing, in the Cold War, to counter East German attempts to unmask bourgeois-capitalist legends and forge an alternative German tradition, 'reeducated' West German professors had various options. Either like Benno von Wiese they offered hugely influential, individual interpretations which purported to be *werkimmanent* asocial and apolitical, but were in fact shot through with familiar old ideological assumptions and value judgements; or, as in Fritz Martini's case,[5] they conceded Poetic-Realists writers' interest in the social dimension of human life but then went on to claim that their true individuality and profundity nonetheless lay elsewhere. Social, liberal concerns allegedly ultimately paled before the consciousness of all-determining uncontrollable, irrational forces like chance and fate. Martini's categories coloured the definitions of German Realism proposed by U.K. scholars. Thus J. M. Ritchie persuasively argued that

---

[4] E. Auerbach, *Mimesis,* (Berne, 1961).

[5] F. Martini, *Deutsche Literatur im bürgerlichen Realismus 1848 - 1898,* (Stuttgart, 1962).

the real strength of the finest Poetic Realists was their evocation of isolated individuals who, unable to find coherence and order in the increasing chaos of the modern world, adopted a resigned, humorous attitude to life's vicissitude and sought a refuge in nature, in the people and in particular cherished regions with their customs and traditions.[6]

The conclusion implicit in Martini's argument was that German culture was not inferior to or distinct from the western-enlightenment tradition: it encompassed and then transcended it with its unique *Innerlichkeit* and existentialist 'realism'. Provincialism and traditionalism were reinstated on a higher plane as defences against the *Angst* and despair of a mechanistic, atomistic modern world. Existentialist views of this type increasingly dominated in the west throughout the 1960s. Given the East-German presence, it was also necessary for Martini to separate the Poetic Realists from pre-1848 radical-revolutionary writers and often from their own beginnings in the Vormärz. His literary history did much to consolidate the view that 1848 was the crucial watershed. German realism was *bürgerlicher Realismus*; its emergence depended on the abandonment of radical aspirations; its socio-economic ideal was compatible with that of the CDU-led German Federal Republic. Friedrich Sengle's later erection of the period 1815-1848 into an entity quite distinct from post-1848 realism reinforced this trend.[7] In Richard Brinkmann's influential work Poetic Realism tended to fragment into individual writers' highly subjective visions of reality,[8] while Wolfgang Preisendanz' emphasis on *Verklärung* and *Humor* as a narrative principle softened and bluntened any critical cutting edge Poetic Realism might have had.[9] The notion gained credence that the 'Poetic' in Poetic Realism denoted a conscious refusal on the part of writers privately pessimistic and disillusioned about life, to express such a view in art. To be palatable or bearable, reality had to be 'poeticised'.

What should now be very clear is that the common denominators postulated by critics over the last one hundred and fifty years tended to move within fairly narrow parameters. The conflicting camps' fortunes swung this way and that, but essentially the debate revolved round a relatively small number of familiar issues.

---

6 J. M. Ritchie, 'Realism' in J. M. R., *Periods in German Literature*, (London, 1966), pp. 171 - 95.

7 F. Sengle, *Biedermeierzeit*, (Stuttgart, 1971ff.)

8 R. Brinkmann, *Wirklichkeit und Illusion*, (Tübingen, 1957).

9 W. Preisendanz, *Humor als dichterische Einbildungskraft. Studien zur Erzählkunst des poetischen Realismus*, (Munich, 1963).

In my view, many of these old categories and perspectives often obscure individual authors' distinctive concerns and techniques; nor, at a more general level, do they do justice to the complex ways in which authors writing in German from the 1840s to the 1890s responded to the challenges posed by their very different states and societies. I certainly think we should scrap any notion of an unlinear, common tradition, of a national literature inspired by a Goethean model. Poetic Realism draws on a much wider national and international culture, both past and present. Sterne, Thackeray, Dickens, for instance, constitute powerful literary models. Can we continue to follow the Prusso-German tradition and exclude Austrian writers, at least after 1866? If Poetic Realism did not flourish in Austria, why? Can we assume that Swiss authors like Keller or Meyer were in literary-cultural terms German nationals? Even within the German states we are dealing with huge regional differences, distinct literary and cultural traditions. With the Prussianisation of Germany north of the Main after 1866 and the creation of a single Imperial market for books and periodicals, the differences remain. I would argue that Poetic Realism's provincialism is not myopic, particularist and that deep, affectionate understanding of a region does not preclude searching criticism of it. Writers' rootedness in particular regions and societies was often a strength rather than a weakness. Especially after the Prussianisation of Germany and the official enthronement of a Social-Darwinist, neo-Hegelian ideology a strong sense of one's regional identity and of very different models and patterns of development constituted a means of preserving alternative traditions. Provincialism provided yardsticks with which to judge the present. The Poetic Realists are not be confused with later *Regional-/Heimatdichter*.

Writers like Keller, Storm, Raabe, Meyer and Fontane exhibit striking affinities in their ideological, moral, social and political concerns. Indeed it would be surprising had not writers who were more or less 'contemporaries' been preoccupied by the great issues, trends and debates of their time. It needed all the ideological and aesthetic manipulations of later generations of critics to convince us otherwise. Whatever the differences in their socio-political analyses and emphases, these writers all share common liberal-humanitarian standards.

One of the corner-stones of Poetic Realism and one of the great common denominators is surely the shared belief in *Humanität*. Achieving it depended on the structure and complexion of state and society. The latter moulded individuals' identity and determined their prospects of happiness and fulfilment. Literature therefore had to play a key role in promoting the emergence of humane institutions and norms. Poetic Realists did not conceive of the self and society, the subjective and the objective as distinct entities. They did not believe that one could or should ignore or transcend the social world in order to explore private worlds and build private refuges. Poetic Realism's strength is that it is social through and through.

All the Poetic Realists had to face the challenge of trying to fill the vacuum left by the failure to reinstate Christian orthodoxy after 1815. Even the most diluted, liberal forms of Protestantism could not resist the all-enveloping atheism. By erecting 1848 as the great caesura and thereby neutralising Vormärz trends, literary historians obscured the extent to which a fervently held belief in the advent of a post-Christian age continued to inspire writers well into subsequent decades. One of the hallmarks of Poetic Realism is that it is premised on a non-theist, god-less reality. Miracles, revelations, signs or symbols do not point to another, higher realm. That is why Stifter should be set apart from the Poetic Realists even if he uses many of the same techniques. Ludwig Feuerbach was a much more important inspiration than Schopenhauer. The finiteness and 'naturalness' of mortal, human life became the great challenge. It brought with it new possibilities, new responsibilities. Writers recognised the need to revise norms and expectations. As they sought artistic means of conveying the divinity of human life, nature, love, etc., *Verklärung* was often a very real attempt to transfigure reality in a quasi-religious way. Essentially Poetic Realism was based on an optimistic understanding of people's potential as natural, human beings. What is so satisfying about the best Poetic-Realist works is their struggle to accommodate the inevitable human experiences of isolation, suffering, ageing, transitoriness and death within the new scheme. The attempt from the later 1860s onwards to safeguard *Humanität* against the new Prusso-German state ideology and the conclusions suggested by science by modifying and extending it gives Poetic-Realist fiction real ethical and intellectual substance, a dynamic inner tension. Writers were prepared to subject humanitarian ideals to the most penetrating scrutiny, to go to the very brink.

And yet the truly common denominator linking the Poetic Realists - the basis of both their finest achievements and their limitations - is their belief in the unique identity of Art. All of them had to contend with insistent claims, either that the writer had been made redundant by the philosopher, the politician, the historian, the entrepreneur or the scientist, or that he/she should put art at the service of these other disciplines and activities. Only by adopting realistic, practical concerns could art, in this view, claim any legitimacy in the modern age. The Poetic

Realists, in contrast, upheld its autonomy, its *Reichsunmittelbarkeit*. While this did not imply any necessary incompatibility between art and other disciplines, art had to remain distinct from them. It could and should incorporate matter from these fields, but it had to do it in and on its own terms. [10] Poetic-Realist writers were often well read in politics, philosophy, history, sociology and science. Yet because they were not prepared to utilise in a raw state concepts and terminology derived from these disciplines and instead insisted on translating them into scenes, sequences and symbols, subsequent critics imagined that the unassuming, unpretentious surface of so many of their works denoted superficiality, an un- or anti-intellectual stance. The Poetic Realists, in contrast, believed that only by relying on its own specific strengths and resources, could art effectively transmit insights and ideals derived from other disciplines. Indeed, if it did so, it constituted the most effective medium in which to communicate them. This faith - and a faith it was - relied on the old trinity of the good, the true and the beautiful and the supposed pre-established harmony between them. The longer the century went on, the more this identity in separateness, this interlocking universe came under strain. In the long run the Poetic Realists were fighting a losing battle to save what was, after all, a historical construct. On the one hand, they were stoutly seeking to prevent this universe disintegrating; on the other, by introducing new themes and ideas, especially naturalist ones, they themselves were massively increasing the pressures it had to endure. Simply in terms of its linguistic prescriptions, this aesthetic had reached its limits. Yet to the very end - *credo quia absurdum* - the Poetic Realists still hoped that art could assimilate and naturalise asylum seekers, could make them subjects in its kingdom rather than it in theirs. 'Wider still and wider etc.' still seemed the best form of imperialist defence for this threatened aesthetic.

One has to concede, too, that the Poetic Realists' tendency to use pictorial, concrete images, scenes and sequences rather than commentaries and authorial glosses did entail limitations. But one should at the same time emphasise the rich possibilities this technique afforded and the strengths it promoted. It certainly did not denote intellectual limitations. We may no longer believe in the Poetic Realists' theories either about artistic creation or about the impact and reception of works of art, but we should recognise that they did give writers the confidence and the courage to believe literature could perform an invaluable role even in the most

---

[10] See D. A. Jackson, *Theodor Storm. The Life and Works of a Democratic Humanitarian*, (Oxford, 1992), pp. 228ff.

inauspicious circumstances.

Fictional works where the intellectual content is to the fore, where authorial commentary and analysis are prominent, may flatter our self-importance as readers but they encourage laziness, keep us minors. We are led round by the hand or nose, continually told how we are to view characters and developments. In the estimation of Poetic Realists, writers needing to do that had shirked or botched the real challenge facing a writer. They had not performed the real miracle, the transmutation of Life into Art. The finest Poetic-Realist works demand very attentive readers. One has to be alert to all the cues and piece together what the great unmentionable, F. R. Leavis, used to call 'the pattern of significances'. These works do not invite slack, indulgent empathy, do not encourage uncritical confirmation in ideological dogmas. Storm spoke of works achieving something midway between *Erschütterung* and *Rührung*; the reader would, he hoped, be left 'in einer herben Nachdenklichkeit über die Dinge des Lebens'. [11]

In genre terms the real achievements of the Poetic Realists lie in the novel and short story. The fact that the latter enjoyed such a lowly status and was unencumbered by precedents and prescriptions meant that it proved much less inhibiting, much more flexible than the epic, drama or lyric. Although recent criticism has explored its formal virtuosity, many discussions of form still tend to depart from models found in classical rhetoric: they regard form as a garment, an adornment or decoration. Devices like the framework narrators, symbols, and parallel plots become the means by which reality was 'poeticised'. In my view the Poetic Realists had a far more organic sense of form. For them the form was inseparable from the content. The form was identical with the message. The view of reality conveyed by Storm's *Auf dem Staatshof*, Meyer's *Der Heilige* or Raabe's *Stopfkuchen* does not exist independently of the form and structure. Having been told on so many occasions that German Poetic Realists are inferior to the English realist novelists, it is gratifying to find late-Victorian champions of modernism urging novelists to adopt techniques which the Poetic Realists had long been applying. Even isolated early Victorians had voiced such demands. Thus Browning wrote to Elisabeth Barrett: 'You speak out, *you* - I only make men and women speak - I give you truth broken into prismatic hues. I fear the

---

[11] Th. Storm to E. Schmidt, September 1881, in *Theodor Storm - Erich Schmidt. Briefwechsel*, ed. K.-E. Laage, (Berlin, 1972ff.), II, 76.

pure white light, even if it is in me.' [12] Some of the finest Poetic-Realist works rely on just this rejection of the insistent, omniscient authorial voice. The tale is told by fictional narrators with a restricted, partial view of things, a false consciousness. Far from being a purely formal device, this technique captured writers' keen awareness of competing ideologies, their growing scepticism about a single road to Enlightenment and Truth along which humanity was irresistibly marching. They recognised as well as any modernist and post-modernist writer that individuals construct their individual realities in terms of their upbringing, prejudices, needs and interests. They also recognised that in their alienation people constructed reality in ways encouraged by dominant social interests and forces. But the Poetic Realists rarely dissolved reality into total, subjective relativity, into 'agnostic' poly-perspectivism. Their stories are normally still constructed to suggest certain fundamental values - even if they escape the fictional narrator or the protagonists. Only rarely, for instance in Meyer's *Der Heilige*, does the form invite the reader to share Hans the bowman's opinion that in judging as in shooting, everything depends on one's standpoint.[13]

Is it Christian love or hatred and resentment of the champions of English and French realism when one finds oneself sharing Virginia Woolf's frustration: 'Begin by saying that her father kept a shop in Harrogate. Ascertain the rent. Ascertain the wages of shop assistants in the year 1878. Discover what her mother died of. Describe cancer. Describe calico. Describe -. But I said: Stop! Stop! And I regret to say that I threw that ugly, that clumsy, that incongruous tool out of the window.' [14] The Poetic Realists never confused Art and Life. They did not imagine that it could or should be equated with science, sociology or photography. It did not offer studies, diagnoses, experiments, Facts.

One final point. Critics have often ignored the varied pressures to which Poetic-Realist writers, like any other writers in any age, were subject. In considering why, for example, radical political views are rarely articulated directly, they ignore both the Poetic Realists' aesthetic principles and the closely related fact that censorship and press laws inevitably affected presentational strategies. Equally if not more significant for subject matter and presentation were the pressures on authors, publishers, and editors, if they were to survive in a

---

[12] Quoted in P. Keating, *The Haunted Study*, (London, 1989), p. 395.

[13] C. F. Meyer, *Sämtliche Werke*, ed. H. Zeller and A. Zäch, (Berne, 1958ff.), XIII, 24.

[14] Quoted in Keating, op. cit., p. 289.

competitive, commercial market, not to antagonise and alienate their readers. One can argue that the growth of the large family magazines made writers more timorous and conformist, made them avoid tabu topics or tone down their presentations. Equally one could argue that as the Wilhelminian middle classes moved further and further from democratic, even liberal-enlightened norms, writers whose fees depended on their favour, had no alternative but to adjust to the new mood. While these constraints undoubtedly took their toll, they did also encourage an artistic subtlety which writers working in a more liberal, permissive climate would perhaps not have elaborated. Only, for example, by using the historical novella so skilfully and by exploiting the resources afforded by complex narrative perspectives could writers like C. F. Meyer in *Die Hochzeit des Mönchs* or *Die Richterin* tackle tabu sexual topics. Whereas mid-Victorian novelists either shared their readers' norms and tabus or accepted the unwritten law that sex should be kept out of modern realist fiction, writers exploiting the possibilities of Poetic Realism could create for themselves the space in which to treat such topics. Victorian realist fiction is often woefully transparent; the Poetic Realists, in contrast, often had to go to work much more stealthily, much more artistically, using all kinds of masks and cloaks. That was the only way of eluding readers' moral sensors and manoeuvring them towards new positions. If Poetic Realism could not tackle certain issues directly head on, it could broach topics unthinkable in middle-class drawing rooms - provided that the rules of art were respected and provided that it allowed its readers a considerable latitude of interpretation. That precondition safeguarded but also limited its critical, humanitarian stance. Here, as in so many other areas, its strength was at the same time its weakness.

# Poetic (symbolic) Realism versus 'l'effet de réel'?

# German nineteenth-century Prose Fiction in its European Context

by Martin Swales

In a justly celebrated essay, Roland Barthes draws our attention to an omnipresent rhetorical device which, for him, is the alpha and omega of nineteenth-century European realism.[1] This - as he calls it - 'effect of the real' consists in repeated gestures of acknowledgement of the physical, material realm, in a ceaseless readiness to describe the palpable world not for its more-than-palpable (that is, higher, or, as we might say, symbolic) potentiality - but for the sake of what it unashamedly is: unregenerate matter. The opening of any Balzac or Dickens novel would provide an admirable illustration of what he means. The details in the Maison Vauquer do not play any role which demands that they be other than or more than themselves, that they signify beyond the common indication. The rhetoric of referentiality is all. The world is the realistic novelist's and all the things that dwell therein. The description of the material world amounts to a subscription to it.

---

[1] R. Barthes, 'L'Effet de réel' in *Littérature et réalité*, ed. G. Genette and T. Todorov, (Paris, 1982), pp. 81 - 90.

If one asks why things, objects, simply acknowledged materiality are so important to the realistic enterprise, the answer must surely be that the traditional realistic novel persistently uncovers the material conditions of (and on) human experience. The material world is not background to the human foreground; rather, there is but one ground. Ontology becomes, we might say, an environmental science. (At which point no doubt, Heidegger turns smartly in his grave).

Because this ground of being is there - as it were in its own right and not for its symbolic import - it follows that nineteenth-century European realism tends to be, in David Lodge's terms, borrowed from Jakobsen, metonymic rather than powerfully metaphorical [2] - unproblematically, transparently referential, that is, rather than strenuously, sustainedly symbolic. All of which suggests two conclusions:

(i)       That the realistic novel does not avidly generate and depend upon symbolic writing.

(ii)      Where it does work figuratively, the implication is that the characters' inwardness is largely imprinted by and requisitioned by the outwardness of practical affairs, of social living. That is to say, the intimations are generated metonymically rather than metaphorically. That much, broadly speaking, would be true, I suspect, of Charles Bovary's cap, of the agricultural fair and Binet's lathe in *Madame Bovary*, of the brothel in *L'Education sentimentale*, of the law courts in *Bleak House*, the debtors' prison in *Little Dorrit*, the school in *Hard Times* (think, for example, of F. R. Leavis' famous discussion), of the train at the end of *Anna Karenina*. Any symbol derives its working, of course, from the interplay of palpable fact and mental creativity, of concrete circumstance and spiritual response. In traditional realistic fiction, the symbols frequently bespeak the metonymic sense that the mind is a social datum, a conditioned, imprisoned entity. The symbols are, more often than not, the precipitate of mental entrapment. (They are not entirely dissimilar in this respect to the Freudian case history where the recurrence of traumatic fears precipitates itself in the baleful re-appearance of symbolic constellations - the fear of windows, trains, hat stands, doors, or whatever. The neurotic fetish is a form of symbol, a symbol of entrapment).

---

[2] D. Lodge, *Modes of Modernist Writing*, (Ithaca/London, 1977), esp. pp. 73 - 124.

In the context of such issues, German prose literature has often been held to be pretty marginal - or, indeed, marginally pretty. Let me recapitulate briefly arguments that are too well known for them to need rehearsing at any length:

(i)     Because of the provincialism, the *Kleinstaaterei* that is so constitutive of 'der deutsche Sonderweg', the social world that is, as it were, available to the German prose writer for artistic re-creation and exploration is small in scope. It tends to result in a little picture, an idyll rather than a panorama of extensive, teeming, bustling life.

(ii)     The lack of human, social, and hence thematic extensiveness is made up for by an intensiveness of artistic treatment whereby modest facts, doings and circumstances yield a significance far in excess of their concrete particularity. Such a constellation is, of course, inherently symbolic - and is metaphorical rather than metonymic.

(iii)     Moreover, as the theory of German nineteenth-century realism, with its concern to distil poetry from prose, value from facticity tells us, such symbolisations are essentially benign and validatory and transfiguring rather than partaking of mechanisms of mental entrapment by social contexts. In this benignity a legacy from classical aesthetics (Goethe and Schiller) and from idealist aesthetics (Hegel) is sustained well into the European age of prosy realism. In the centrality of symbolisations within German prose, we are - so the traditional view runs - at the very heart of Poetic (ie German) realism in contradistinction to Prosaic (ie European) Realism. The key tenets can be heard in Erich Heller's discussion of Goethe's 'realism of the symbol' as understood by Nietzsche: 'The realism of the symbol becomes that artistic vindication of the beauty of a lovable world.'[3] Or, to take another example, (and this is Heller *in propria persona*):

> What I mean by true order? An order that embodies the incalculable and unpredictable, transcending our rational grasp precisely where it meets the reasons of the heart. The symbol is the body of that which transcends, the measure of the immeasurable, and the visible logic of the heart's reasoning.[4]

This is the almost eucharistic notion of the symbol, one which Walter Benjamin

---

[3] E. Heller, *The Disinherited Mind*, (Harmondsworth, 1961), p. 96.

[4] Ibid, p. 257.

challenged in his defence of allegory in the *Ursprung des deutschen Trauerspiels*.

All this is, as I have suggested, a very German tradition of aesthetic-cum-cultural thinking, and it finds its correlative in a tradition of realistic writing that is, compared to that produced by the rest of Europe, not only insistently but also benignly (eucharistically) symbolic, transfigurative of material experience, more than merely metonymic. And yet: for all its seriousness and nobility, this narrative tradition is, on the traditional view, little better than a backwater, part of that 'fatale deutsche Innerlichkeit' that goes with the existence of a 'Kulturnation' in lieu of the modern 'politische Nation'. Here again we touch on the clichés and standard assumptions in respect of the cultural, social, political life of Germany from the late eighteenth century to the catastrophes of the first half of the twentieth.

Now there is a measure of truth to such arguments, I think. But in certain respects they have to be challenged. One particularly damaging orthodoxy is the dismissal of all German contributions to literary realism because of their inwardness and reflectivity. Such knee-jerk thinking rests on a norm of thinking about realism that is (like so many norms) unreflected and simplistic. In my view, a number of developments in recent critical theory have challenged the notion of realism as simple unmediated referentiality, of realism as transparency upon an extra-textual world.[5] I have no wish to be modish; but the challenge is important and it enables one to differentiate the notion of how literary realism can work. And it allows us to respond more adequately to certain works of German fiction and to incorporate them into that concern, so characteristic of literature of the European nineteenth century, to comprehend human experience as something inalienably housed in the nexus of social relations.

I want to be brief in my consideration of these theoretical issues. My overriding aim is to suggest that there is such a thing as a realism of mental life, of mentality and discourse. If Balzac, Dickens, and Flaubert are unforgettable in their portrayal of the physical furniture of any given period, the German tradition may be supreme in its understanding of the mental furniture of an age.

The theoretical issues which I would mention are:

(i)     Facts, within the human context, are not simple materiality, not unmediated thereness. Rather, they are physical entities invested with meaning, rendered significant, intelligible. In this sense, then, 'il n'y a pas de hors-texte'.

---

[5] See C. Prendergast, *The Order of Mimesis*, (Cambridge, 1986) and L. R. Furst, *Realism*, (London, 1992).

(ii)     Literature is made of language. It can, therefore, only produce a replica of discourse about the material world, not a replica of materiality as such. One is reminded of Magritte's wonderfully realistic depiction in paint on canvas of a pipe, under which he writes: 'Ceci n'est pas une pipe.'

(iii)     If the sofa in a Balzac novel is made of words and not of leather and horsehair, it follows that there is, in the traditional realistic novel, a disjunction between the medium of the social datum and that of its literary exploration. But this is not true if the social datum is a mental entity - is the values, conventions, assumptions, perceptions, symbols, clichés of the institutionalised subjectivity of an age.

I want now to refer to particular texts, to indicate briefly the operative nexus of symbolisation within certain works of German prose and to suggest that those symbolisations are not transcendental negations of social life but rather the mode of its artistic re-creation, negotiation, and, ultimately, interrogation.

Let me add one further theoretical reflection before coming to the discussion of specific texts. And it has to do with the question as to whose consciousness finds expression in the symbolisations that are so important. What I shall want to suggest is that at one level the characters do comprehend, perceive, and on occasion make the symbols that govern their lives; but, at another level, the symbols are enacted rather than comprehended by the characters - and in such cases we, the readers, understand whereas the characters may not. In that dialectic of witting and unwitting, of comprehension and incomprehension expressed by the symbol is to be found both the freedom and the unfreedom, both the dignity and the entrapment that characterise the soul of men and women living in the nexus of social relations.

I want to begin with Gottfried Keller, with *Romeo und Julia auf dem Dorfe*. A glance at the secondary literature devoted to this story will confirm that all commentators have perceived the extraordinary symbolic density of its whole narrative strategy. The crucial question is: what does that symbolic density achieve?

At one level, as the title itself suggests, we are concerned with a contemporary *village* version of the *Romeo and Juliet* story. In Keller's world, in accordance with the 'Dialektik der Kulturbewegung', the Shakespearean destiny written in the heavens, that of the 'star cross'd lovers', modulates into the socio-economic and cultural, in a word *communal*, destiny of two young people whose fate is unambiguously sealed here on earth and nowhere else - in the lovers' internalisation of the sights and sounds, of the recurrent conventions and practices of their social world. The way of life in which they grow up enshrines security and strength - but also desperate entrapment. They themselves both see and do not see how the processes that sustain them become the terrible engine that destroys them - and this is true of their families as well. The pattern of knowing and not knowing is there in the justly famous ploughing scene which opens the *Novelle*. At one level, the farmers Manz and Marti know what they are doing as they plough back and forth, remorselessly shaving the extra furrow from the disputed land between them. Their attitudes become abundantly apparent in the conversation between them when they stop for lunch. Yet a narratorial comment such as 'so gehen die Weberschiffchen des Geschickes aneinander vorbei und "was er webt, das weiß kein Weber"!' [6] which echoes the earlier simile of the farmers' movements being 'wie zwei untergehende Gestirne' (p. 87) sets up an intimation of fatality to which clearly they themselves are blind. Years later, when the lovers are first reunited after the years of feuding and decline which have devastated both their families, they arrange to meet in precisely the territory of that opening scene - in that symbolic site of the orderliness that means so much to them. Clearly they know what they are doing when they go there - and in part they know why they are doing it. But when they walk hand in hand in the patterns of their fathers' ploughing, they are oblivious to the symbolic process which they confirm. But the narrator makes sure that we understand:

> ... sie legten zwei oder dreimal den Hin- und Herweg zurück, still, glückselig und ruhig, so daß dieses eine Paar nun auch einem Sternbilde glich, welches über die sonnige Rundung der Anhöhe und hinter derselben niederging, wie einst die sicher gehenden Pflugzüge ihrer Väter. (p. 129)

The key metaphorical nexus in the story of 'wild', 'Wildnis', 'verwildert', 'Verwilderung' is deeply enmeshed in - and expressive of - social categories of orderliness and transgression, categories that are implanted in the socialised consciousness of the characters. Even the moments that are mysterious or uncanny - like the various appearances of the Black Fiddler - partake of a socially

---

[6] G. Keller, *Sämtliche Werke*, ed. J. Fränkel, (Zurich and Munich, 1926ff.). *Romeo und Julia auf dem Dorfe* is to be found in Vol. VII, 84 - 187, here 96. Subsequent references are included in the text.

generated thematic of the known and the unknown, the familiar and the unsettling. (Much the same is true, I would suggest, of the Chinaman in Fontane's *Effi Briest*). The lovers know that they can only be happy in a blameless marriage, in a life lived 'auf einem guten Grund und Boden'. The existential metaphorics vibrate with the socio-cultural specificity of the ploughing scene, of that 'Grund und Boden' that is the alpha and omega of the story. In a rare moment of self-analysis, Sali speaks for the intensely socialised consciousness and conscience of their love when he recognises that the two of them can run away from the Black Fiddler but not from themselves: 'Diesen sind wir entflohen ... aber wie entfliehen wir uns selbst? Wie meiden wir uns?' (p. 181) Keller's incomparable story perceives that there is no self other than what they have and are; and what they have and are is made by the socio-economic specificity of mid-nineteenth-century Switzerland. The aesthetic patterns, the symbolic coherences of Keller's narrative uncover the recurrent destiny of socio-psychological motivations within the lives of the fictional characters, motivations of which they are but partially aware.

A similar interlocking of socio-psychological and aesthetic issues informs Keller's novel *Der grüne Heinrich*. Both as character and as narrator (and I should make clear that I am concerned here with the second version of the novel) Heinrich Lee constantly reflects on the ways and means by which art conveys the nature of extra-literary and extra-painterly experience. The intensity of reflectivity and reflection entails not a transcendence of the social world but critical engagement with it. Keller constantly reminds us that what human beings inhabit and experience as reality is not unmediated facts but facts informed by innumerable acts of reflection and interpretation. At this level, the artistic medium (the symbolisations of the work of art) interlocks with extra-novelistic reality because, in human affairs, 'il n'y a pas de hors-texte'.

There are four key strands to this crucial overlap of literary, artistic medium and social event:

(i)     The theme of the social role of art, popular taste, Habersaat's studio for the mass production of landscapes, all of which foreground the issue of art as social commodity.

(ii)     Heinrich's frequent attempts, rendered with much detail and particularity, to replicate the physical world in his painting.

(iii)     The symbolisations of communal life - the *Wilhelm Tell* pageant in the village and the medieval pageant in Munich.

(iv)     The religious theme and the erotic theme also raise and focus the issue of the relationship between mind and matter, between imagination and facticity. And that theme informs both the events of the novel and its first-person narrative mode. European realism has no shortage of novels in which the imaginative selfhood of the youthful hero collides with the unyielding world of material and social palpability. One thinks of (among other examples) *Le Rouge et le Noir, David Copperfield, The Way of All Flesh, Jude the Obscure*. Yet none of these novels takes philosophical and cognitive issue with the nature and modality of the relationship between the imaginative potential of the individual and the sheer thereness of the material world with the thoughtfulness and subtlety of Keller's novel. Its symbols are both the stuff of its thematic statement and the object of narrative reflection. The interplay of past, experiencing self and now, narrating self accounts for an especially intense interplay of insight and perception, of conscious and unconscious symbolisation.

In an entirely remarkable passage Heinrich as narrator reflects that what conjoins art and social reality is the capacity for creating and inhabiting fictions. Reference is made to 'revalenta arabica', a herb which is so vigorously marketed that imaginative fiction becomes operative economic fact:

> Ein Spekulant gerät auf die Idee der Revalenta arabica (so nennt er es wenigstens) und bebaut dieselbe mit aller Umsicht und Ausdauer; sie gewinnt eine ungeheure Ausdehnung und gelingt glänzend; tausende Menschen werden in Bewegung gesetzt und hunderttausende, vielleicht Millionen gewonnen, obgleich jedermann sagt: es ist ein Schwindel![7]

What is particularly remarkable here is the mixture of knowingness and self-delusion, of detachment and surrender which characterises economic reality and, we could add, aesthetic experience. Money, like art, is a form of symbolic currency.

I want to move on to Theodor Fontane. There has been no shortage of critical voices that have seen Fontane as the realistic chronicler par excellence of *gründerzeitlich* Berlin. Yet equally it has often been said that he is too muted and half-hearted to achieve the power and scale of the classics of European realism. I

---

[7] G. Keller, *Sämtliche Werke*, op. cit., VI, 37 - 8.

would wish to argue that the half-heartedness has to do with his thoroughgoing comprehension of the socialised nature of his characters and their experience. Effi Briest speaks for many of his protagonists when she says: 'Es ist komisch, aber ich kann eigentlich von vielem in meinem Leben sagen "beinah".' [8] The 'beinah', the law of 'more or less', 'after a fashion', 'one way or another' is the law of socially caused inauthenticity which so many of Fontane's characters know all too well. Hence his fondness for dialogue, for conversation; even *in extremis*, even in moments of crisis when the characters are thrown back on their own resources, their monologues cannot shed the socially imprinted parole. The monologue is still a dialogue in which the self speaks not to itself but to the social world which it carries round with it. The characters are never proof against the discourse of their social world; they are unemphatic, unassertive - as is the prose of their maker.

This brings me to a key aspect of Fontane's art - to those symbols, those 'Finessen' of which he was so proud and which mean that the primary gesture of seemingly casual, unpurposive eavesdropping on the ways of the world is actually shot through with a sophisticated patterning which gives the reader orientation, perspective, overview. But patterning in aid of what?

The first thing to say is that many of the symbols and leitmotifs have to do with the entrapped condition of the characters. Their recurrence is the measure of the trained, constrained consciousness. Think of the 'Schloon' and the Chinaman in *Effi Briest* which link with the taboo realm which is defined and marginalised by the social concordat, by the force of 'Pakt und Übereinkommen'. [9]

That Fontane was a consummate artist is beyond doubt. However, in an important article Karl S. Guthke raises a dissenting voice in that he vigorously attacks the virtuosity of certain critics (for discerning patterns everywhere) - and the (as he sees it) irritating structural virtuosity of Fontane himself. [10] Guthke objects that some of the symbolic intimations are too knowing - they are over-emphatic to the point of portentousness. What I think Guthke overlooks is the interplay of consciousness and unconsciousness in the symbolisations of the Fontane text. Many of the symbols derive from the mental processes of the characters themselves and are for this reason explicit. At times they perceive the

---

[8] Th. Fontane, *Werke, Schriften und Briefe*, ed. W. Keitel and H. Nürnberger, (Munich, 1962ff.), IV, 280.

[9] Th. Fontane, *Schriften zur Literatur*, ed. H. H. Reuter, (Berlin, 1960), p. 185.

[10] K. S. Guthke, 'Fontanes "Finessen" - "Kunst" oder "Künstelei"?', *JDSG*, 26 (1982), 235 - 61.

extent of their own entrapment, of their own indwelling in inescapably recurrent patterns, and then they express themselves in an overt, even self-stylising, recognition of their own condition. This, I would suggest, is true of Botho's final utterance in *Irrungen Wirrungen* which provides the closing cadence of the novel (and to which Guthke objects). Botho's wife Käthe notices the announcement of an engagement in the morning paper. She finds the names - Gideon Franke and Lene Nimptsch - comic. But her husband replies that Gideon is after all better than Botho. Clearly Botho knows what he is saying here. At one level he remains within the genial workability of his marriage to Käthe, and his tone is one of willed harmlessness at the breakfast table. But the subtext vibrates with the full - and hurtful - extent of his deprivation. Similarly Lene's flowers, the 'Immortellen', her reference to hair that binds, Botho's farewell to the love letters in the fire - 'alles Asche. Und *doch* gebunden' [11] - these symbolic moments form a nexus of signification which the characters themselves establish. They are overtly signs and portents, perceived and uttered or thought as such by the characters.

But many of the moments of symbolisation are unconscious. The motif of 'so was' in *Effi Briest* is supremely an example of this. [12] The 'Effi komm' is both conscious and unconscious. Effi's playmates use the phrase artlessly; but Innstetten registers the words as a kind of omen. When the phrase recurs in the father's telegram, there can, surely, be no question of a knowing recollection of the brief incident of many years previously. But *we* make the link; and thereby we consider and reflect on modes of socialisation within the family. It is precisely the interplay of knowing and not knowing, of the overt and the subliminal, of revelation and concealment that is central to the manifold ways in which Fontane's technique of aesthetic, novelistic symbolisation parallels and articulates the symbolisations of the socialised psyche. Many of Fontane's characters may have resigned themselves to societal imperatives; but that resignation is not a condition of engulfing Pavlovian acquiescence. Rather, it is a process of deprivation that is lived through daily and that sometimes surfaces to consciousness. And that mechanism of repression and acknowledgement is at the heart of Fontane's symbolic 'Finessen'. Fontane is incomparable in his understanding of the ways in which, and the extent to which, socialisation both contributes to and takes a terrible toll of human happiness.

---

[11] Th. Fontane, *Werke, Schriften und Briefe*, op. cit., II, 455.

[12] See E. Swales, 'Private Mythologies and Public Unease. On Fontane's *Effi Briest*', *MLR*, 75 (1980), 114 - 23.

Something similar applies to the fiction of Wilhelm Raabe. I want to confine my remarks to *Pfisters Mühle*. The mill is the scene of the events portrayed, and it is also the place in which, in the course of a summer holiday, Ebert Pfister writes the account that we are reading. The mill's history expresses larger processes of socio-economic change: initially in the eighteenth century, it is central to the agrarian productivity of the area, then, in the first half of the nineteenth century, it becomes a place of leisure, a tavern run by Ebert's father - and now (in the latter part of the nineteenth century) an obsolete relic, sold off to the sugar beet processing factory upstream that pollutes the water with effluent. Because of the doom hanging over the mill, the summer which Ebert and his young wife Emmy spend there will be their last in the parental home. They live in Berlin - but for Ebert the mill is the childhood idyll, and he resents having to lose it. Both voluntarily and involuntarily, memories come back to him - and with those memories pictures from and symbols of a different world. One phrase recurs with obsessive regularity throughout Ebert's account. It is: 'wo bleiben alle die Bilder?'[13] In it he expresses regret at the loss of an idyllic world, a world replete with symbols and signs - and regret at the coming of a new, functional, factual world, one sustained either by no symbols at all, or, if by symbols, then by negative ones (the factory chimneys on the road to Berlin, for example). Emmy knows the dangers inherent in such a mentality, dangers that can lead to a fixation on the past and a devaluation of the present. She constantly interrupts the flow of Ebert's writing, and with it the flow of his nostalgia, by summoning him down from his study. Moreover she countermands his nostalgic images of the past with images of the fulfilment and happiness of their life in Berlin - and of the splendid vigour and openness of the bustling capital city. The battle of symbols in the narrative enacts the socio-psychological battle in Ebert as he confronts the loss of an older world and the ebullient emergence of a new and very different one. Above all, Emmy insists that the symbols of the past do not expand to become subliminally operative (and therefore emotionally and cognitively unchallengeable) tributes to irretrievable loss. She obliges Ebert to make those symbols explicit, to hold them up to conscious scrutiny - and to recognise that the idyllic world was not a haven of perfection, but a prison for many of their friends, for Adam and Albertine in particular. The battle of the symbols in Ebert's account is the battle for a just and unsentimental comprehension of the pain and the necessity of socio-economic change.

---

13 W. Raabe, *Sämtliche Werke*, ed. K. Hoppe, (Göttingen, 1951ff.), XVI, 30f.

I come finally to Thomas Mann's *Buddenbrooks*. It is, of course, a novel that is manifestly, even claustrophobically, symbolic in its aesthetic organisation. But this is not simply the result of virtuosity on Mann's part. The novel follows the fortunes of a family over three generations, and in the process it attends to the intense symbolisations of traditional family ritual with which the Buddenbrooks fill their lives. The novel registers the shift of values, the disturbance of mentality that goes with the social and economic changes between the 1830s and the 1870s. And as the mentality shifts, so the symbols and rituals become problematic. The successive generations of Buddenbrooks become more reflective and thoughtful, and as they come to think, so they reflect on the symbolic structure that is at the heart of the tradition which they are being asked to sustain. The symbols by which they are required to live are scrutinised and found wanting. These symbols are as much part of their way of life as the furniture on which they sit. The Buddenbrooks are what they are by virtue of the physical and mental furniture that defines and shapes their lives. And the novel is faithful to both kinds of furniture, reflecting them, and, as the Buddenbrooks come to question and brood, reflecting on them. We as readers know what Thomas Buddenbrook means when he bitterly reflects that symbols, once they are entrusted to his care, once they are dependent on him for their safe keeping, become either brittle or so much unendurable dead weight:

> ... es kam die Senatswahl, und ich hatte Glück, und hier wuchs das Haus aus dem Erdboden. Aber 'Senator' und 'Haus' sind Äußerlichkeiten, und ich weiß etwas, woran du noch nicht gedacht hast, ich weiß es aus Leben und Geschichte. Ich weiß, daß oft die äußeren, sichtbarlichen und greifbaren Zeichen und Symbole des Glückes und Aufstieges erst erscheinen, wenn in Wahrheit alles schon wieder abwärts geht. [14]

In his anguish, Thomas monitors the flux and change of his own and his family's fortunes in the symbolic terms that the novel itself puts before us. In respect of both the characters' being and the artistic being of the novel in which they figure, self-consciousness and reflectivity are part of historicity, part of the novel's realism.

It is important, then, to see the symbolic density of *Buddenbrooks* not as some aesthetic transfiguration of social reality, not as the sacramental validation of a lovable world, but rather as the aesthetic mode by which a given society is both

---

[14] Th. Mann, *Gesammelte Werke*, (Frankfurt am Main, 2/1974), I, 431.

re-created and interrogated. At one level, those symbols and patterns bespeak programmed living, the security of unquestioned, conditioned experience, bespeak that interface where the inwardness of the characters interlocks with - and is programmed by - the outwardness of 'being a Buddenbrook'. Yet this is not quite the whole story. Sometimes the symbols express small territories of non-programmed knowing, of genuine cognitive clarity, perhaps even spiritual dignity. Let me illustrate this with reference to Tony.

At one level she is supremely the programmed and self-programming Buddenbrook. She parrots catch-phrases and formulae because she lives a life of imposed and self-imposed obedience to the family ethos. Yet there is, I would suggest, more than parrot-dom to the quotations from the love affair with Morten Schwarzkopf at Travemünde for the crucial reason that they obstinately vibrate with a glimpse of human fulfilment irrevocably forfeited. They constitute a private code to which no-one (apart from us, the readers) is party, a code which keeps alive, in however ritualised or reified a form, a corner of inwardness that is not aligned with the Buddenbrook ethos. Hence it is she who understands better than anybody else Hanno's heartbreak at having to leave Travemünde. She comforts him with the story she had told Morten - how when she was little, she took a large number of jellyfish home in her handkerchief, hoping that, as the water evaporated, the stars would be left behind. But the end result is a damp patch on the balcony: 'Es roch nur ein bißchen nach faulem Seetang ...'[15] The identical phrase is repeated five hundred pages and many years later when she talks to Hanno. The symbolic resonance in the words - to the effect that the freedom and beauty of Travemünde cannot be transported back to Lübeck - speaks of deprivation deeply felt.

The symbols in Buddenbrooks enact the central dialectic which concerns me; they speak of the reassurance of regimented behavioural patterns and of the suffering that derives from that regimentation. In a wonderfully precise distillation of socio-psychological mechanisms, the symbols both reveal and conceal, both acknowledge and repress, both express and regiment the flux of human feelings.

Let me draw my argument to a close. In theoretical terms, I have been suggesting that there is a traditional notion of novel realism which views the novel as the repository of material plenitude and upholds formal looseness and aesthetic sprawl as the correlative of the profuse materiality of the physical world. The result is the 'loose baggy monster' of the untidy but eminently worldly novel of

---

[15] Ibid, 137.

European realism. My argument is that much German fiction is manifestly structured, is through-composed; and that, as a consequence of that intensity of aesthetic patterning, the details and facts become invested with significance beyond their materiality - that is, they become symbols. Yet this formal control, this fondness for symbolic intimation need not be a flight from or a prettification of the social world; rather, it can be its exploration and critique in that it constantly monitors the interface between psychological inwardness and social outwardness. The German novel attends to the reflectivity of its characters, to the limitations placed upon that reflectivity and to the freedom and energy that it retains against all the odds. It also appeals to our reflectivity, asking us to attend to the patterned interplay of symbols in the text - and to the operational force of those symbols in the extra-literary world. This dimension of reflectivity is, I believe, more richly present in the German prose tradition than in the mainstream of European realism. In consequence, there is a greater intensity of symbolic intimation; and there is also a dialectic of symbolic intimation, of revelation and concealment which is legitimately part of the realistic enterprise. My point is not that German prose is better than the European Pantheon; but it is that it does belong in that Pantheon - and not in some sad junk shop of unreadable literature. What has often been held to be the backwardness of German prose may in fact be at the nerve centre of the project of European realism.

**************

As a final footnote I should like to offer one further glimpse of that nerve centre, and I want to change genre and move to drama.

At the end of Ibsen's *Ghosts* the savagely naturalistic, scientific-determinist argument runs its appointed course. The oppressive narrowness of small-town Norwegian society has cankered all joy in living - Mr Alving consorts with prostitutes, and the syphilis that destroys him is passed on to his son, Oswald. As Oswald tries to live out his human and artistic creativity in Bohemian circles in Paris, the illness is diagnosed which spells his doom. He returns home to die. At the end of the play, the living death begins and the mind slips into idiocy. And Oswald repeats a phrase over and over again. The ghastly repetitions express utter entrapment; the determinist agencies of *race, moment, milieu* have triumphed. Oswald's idiocy produces vacant utterances; but it is not rubbish that he speaks. The phrase he utters is not only articulate, it has a desperate poetry to it. 'Give me the sun,' he says. At the heart of the symbolic enactment of entrapment is the symbolic cry for a fuller life. In this luminous and lacerating moment, the whole of nineteenth-century European drama seems to be distilled.

That legacy is carried forward into the twentieth century as the aesthetics of realistic-cum-naturalistic drama collide with the need for a new visionariness that would entail new artistic and human moulds. Hence the Expressionism of the later Ibsen, later Strindberg; hence, Toller, Kaiser, Claudel, T. S. Eliot, Christopher Fry and the David Hare of *Secret Rapture*. But the old, unyielding truths of realism will not go away; with Osborne, Pinter, Ayckbourn the perception of human entrapment is as thoroughgoing as ever. Perhaps this battle for the soul of twentieth-century theatre helps us to see why Bertolt Brecht is so important. His aesthetics of the drama are both to do with realism and to do with distantiation; both to do with acknowledging the entrapment of the characters and of ourselves as powerless onlookers and with creating a site of freedom for the figures on the stage, whereby the illusion is suspended as an actor or actress speaks, articulating what could or might be the characters' reflectivity - and thereby energising our reflectivity.

And what of the symbol in all this? We know how careful Brecht was about things, about props for his theatre. No trace of anti-realism in the choice of bowls, spoons, in the design of Mother Courage's wagon. So, at one level, the things had to stay within their physical signification. A drum is what it is in the Thirty Years War - an item of military equipment, used to summon, to drill, to regiment, and, if symbolic at all, then symbolic of inwardness aligned to the outwardness of military order. Yet in one truly remarkable scene Kattrin takes that item of military furniture, that symbol of conditioning and unfreedom, and hammers out the clamour of her autonomy. The trapped creature - robbed of speech by the war, denied the only fulfilment she has ever wanted (marriage, children), becomes articulate in the way that the trapped Oswald does. In a fearsomely prosaic world, that battering drum is the nearest we get to poetry.

As we reflect on such scenes and on the symbolic nexus of which they are part, we reflect on the profoundest dialectic of literary realism, and on the profoundest issue of the nineteenth century, and of our age too.

# Self-Reflexive Discourse:

# An Aspect of German Realist Writing

by Mark G. Ward

To posit that literature is a self-reflexive phenomenon, that its referentiality is self-referentiality, and that its capacity to generate meaning is dependent on a system of intertexts which not only mark out, but also fundamentally constrain and simultaneously construct the space within which any such meaning can be located, is to make a statement that is at once both underpinned by generations of understanding, and that at the same time challenges central tenets of traditional liberal critical thinking relating to this aspect of human creativity. Moreover, to raise issues of this order in the context of matters relating to Realism, a cultural phenomenon which however difficult of definition, is nevertheless commonly agreed to recognise and attempt to re-present a reality other than itself, the concrete world of palpable, tangible *res* and relations, may seem to be an example of wilful insistence on paying lip service to current issues of critical theory. It is also, of course, to undertake an act of conflation or elision of category, for self-reflexivity, self-referentiality and intertextuality, while arguably possibly generically related, should, nevertheless each be seen as a discrete phenomenon, each with its own theoretical underpinning and each with its own practical consequences. But while for the moment eschewing this kind of distinction, vital as in some contexts it ultimately may be, it is nevertheless the case that examples of writing in German to which the label realist, however qualified, has been attributed do show a quite remarkable degree of at least self-consciousness.

It was, of course, well acknowledged in the nineteenth century that to write in the prose medium was to risk engaging with a medium that was *a priori* unaesthetic and hence the frequent recourse to some kind of introductory framework in which the status of the ensuing narrative was clearly signalled as literary discourse - 'Geschichte', 'erzählen' - fulfilled the function of protecting the narrative from assimilation to other forms of prose writing such as journalism or reportage. Such instances of self-reflexivity or self-consciousness are, however, only one small part of this whole area, and the question would in any case remain as to whether such an explanation of this dimension of self-reflexivity - the establishing of aesthetic identity - is in any way exhaustive of either purpose or effect.

In the case of a work such as *Die Chronik der Sperlingsgasse* the phenomenon of self-consciousness has often been remarked, as indeed it has with regard to the cycle *Die Leute von Seldwyla*, but crucially the area requiring investigation is the matter of what this aspect of self-consciousness or self-reflexivity may be indicative. As is well known, the seminal discussion of Raabe by Barker Fairley had as its underlying strategy a concern to rescue Raabe from the charges of avoiding the thrust of mainstream European realism and dwelling in, to borrow the word from Martin Swales, 'backwaterdom',[1] and with that concern a desire to rehabilitate Raabe by designating him a forerunner of twentieth-century experimental fiction.[2] The *Chronik* is seen constantly to be debating its own status as a novel, indeed to be rejecting that generic classification in favour of a different identity where the perceived strict organisational principles of the novel form do not apply, but rather a looser form of organisation such as that dictated by the more haphazard workings of the individual consciousness and realised in the form of a loose-leaf 'Bilderbogen'. The mediation of reality through, and overtly through, the consciousness of the one narrating figure is seen on the one hand as a reworking of Kantian epistemology, and on the other, or equally perhaps in that capacity, as an anticipation of the principles of neo-romanticism, impressionism and the general fragmentation of the perception of reality which is the hallmark of

---

[1] M. W. Swales, '"Neglecting the Weight of the Elephant ...": German Prose Fiction and European Realism', *MLR*, 83 (1988), 882.

[2] B. Fairley, *Wilhelm Raabe*, (Oxford, 1961).

modernism.[3] The underlying concern here to find a framework of discussion which does justice to the peculiarity of nineteenth-century German prose narrative when compared to the European tradition, while not being forced to interpret that peculiarity as a sign of inferiority - technical accomplishment but failure adequately to render or engage the broad panoramic sweep of socio-historical reality [4] - is a concern that I share. Whether, however, that framework of discussion is best located within the kind of area opened up by Barker Fairley is an open question.

It is admittedly frequently the case that to debate in and around the area of the self-reflexivity of literary discourse is to enter the world of post-structuralism and beyond and to become, in Eagleton's words, 'the critical sceptic sensually thrilling to the unfounded play of signs', that is 'the son of the metaphysical father rapt before the ritual of ultimate meaning'.[5] Self-reflexive writing is seen as writing which foregrounds the awareness of itself as the system within which the conditions are set for the generation of meaning, but a meaning which then has at best validity within that system and which lacks the power to relate to, and/or to articulate, a system other than and outside itself. Within such an understanding 'signification depends not on the correlation of signs with bits of reality but on the order of signs among themselves'[6] - and the text is the system which establishes that order. But devoid of a referent these signs can do no other then reflect back, each upon the other, in an infinite process of mirroring, and through these mirror images achieve differentiation within the bordered system of the text, a bordered system which contains the endless chain of signification, located in nothing other than itself, and endlessly deferring meaning. To pursue this kind of area is, I

---

[3] See, for example, S. Kohl, *Realismus: Theorie und Geschichte*, (Munich, 1977), p. 111: 'Im Werk Raabes zeigt sich beispielhaft für den deutschen Realismus des 19. Jhrdts., wie die Überzeugung von einer erkennbaren Weltharmonie mehr und mehr von Zweifeln bedroht wird und die Darstellung eines "Zusammenhangs der Dinge" nur als subjektive Setzung gelingt.'

[4] A typical judgement can be found in G. J. Becker (ed), *Documents of Modern Literary Realism*, (Princeton, 1963), p.12: 'German participation in the realistic movement leaves much to be desired so far as both critical discussion and the works produced are concerned. Though there were during the middle of the century works of a certain importance in terms of their representation of everyday life, there was also a tendency toward what is called "poetic realism", which inclines toward the sentimental.' The issue is also well addressed by M. Swales, 'The Problem of nineteenth-century German Realism' in *Realism in European Literature*, ed. N. Boyle and M. Swales, (Cambridge, 1986), pp. 68f.

[5] T. Eagleton, *Criticism and Ideology*, (London, 1976), p. 168.

[6] J. Frow, *Marxism and Literary History*, (Oxford, 1986), p. 65.

would suggest, to inhabit a timeless world of ahistorically textual and discursive navel contemplation which may have something of the fascination felt by the mathematician driven on by the internal logic of abstract symbols, but which cannot produce a satisfactory, or satisfying, resolution to the basic hermeneutic drive of the human mind in relation to material which clearly does relate somehow or other to recognisable human experience. It is, at the same time, to inhabit a world which in one sense is incoherent, in that the area of enquiry ignores the very condition which established the method in the first place. For as long as the referent enjoyed idealist status, then the focus, as in classical structuralism, was on the mechanism whereby meaning was generated within a system where that meaning was unproblematic.[7] Means, not end, was in a sense the concern since the end was semantically guaranteed even from the outset, and was moreover guaranteed within an essentially ahistorical context.

It was, as Derrida notoriously pointed out,[8] the historical moment at which the metaphysical, that is idealist, guarantee of truth was withdrawn that set the necessary conditions to postulate the endless free play of signs, the self-reflexive text, the ahistorical self-consciousness, and most importantly a key dimension of that moment has to be the movement of the nineteenth century towards a structure of thought in the materialist mode. The condition for the new kind of metaphysic, indeed quasi-mystical awareness of the impossibility of ultimate truth, truth that has, as it were, come to rest rather than being caught up in a process and hence endlessly mobile and elusive, is then curiously, possibly paradoxically, what might be seen as its logical antithesis, the growing dissemination and acceptance of materialist structures. But this logical contradiction, the possible paradox, may only be relevant if the aspect of self-reflexivity which I believe can be identified in many German texts of the mid- to late- nineteenth century and to which the label realist has conventionally been applied is properly to be seen as part of the internal process of internal mirroring and (self-) reflection. If, on the other hand, the recurrence in so-called realist texts of instances of self-reflexion is seen within parameters other than those of narcissistic and introspective self-absorption, then there may emerge a criterion which on the one hand distinguishes the German tradition from the European - and it must be accepted that the German expression, and experience, of the nineteenth century was in marked ways different - while at

---

[7] See F. Jameson, *The Ideologies of Theory*, (London, 1988), and T. Bennett, *Marxism and Formalism*, (London, 1979), pp. 71ff.

[8] J. Derrida, *Writing and Difference*, transl. with an introduction and additional notes by A. Bass, (London and Henley, 1978), p. 280.

the same time underscoring its ultimately more radically realist basis, where realism is taken to be the explicit awareness of, and exploration of, not only the socio-historical and cultural specificity of an object, but also the awareness of the means and/or process whereby that specificity is created.

For fundamentally the nature of realism as the philosophy which accepts the existence of things independently of the mind and as such occupies the counter-terrain to idealist structures, is an epistemological question, and not a matter of, say, style.[9] Certainly that generation of writers and literati which emerged in the wake of 1848, which saw itself at the forefront of the new realist writing and which felt itself to be charting out the new direction, frequently identified its newness in epistemological terms, specifically in the rejection of idealist premises.[10] Hettner, for example, writing in 1850 remarks:

> Ueberall weht uns der Frühlingshauch frischer Werdelust erquickend entgegen. Ueberall das hastige Drängen, die Kunst aus aller hohlen Idealistik und Phantastik in die Leiden und Freuden, in die Formen und Eigenheiten unserer eigenen Welt hineinzuführen. Unsere junge Literatur kämpft unzweifelhaft, zum Theil mehr als sie selbst weiß, gegen den falschen Idealismus unserer sogenannten Klassiker und Romantiker.[11]

or one could cite Auerbach:

> Der gesunde Realismus ist die Freude an der Welt, an der wirklichen Welt, wo sich immer aus der Erkenntniß auch die Schönheit und Gesetzmäßigkeit offenbart. Der Idealismus, der den Dingen sein subjectives und vorgefaßtes Programm einprägen, Bedingungen setzen will statt die gesetzten zu erfassen, hat die Schwärmerei und Blasirtheit zu Zwillingssöhnen.[12]

The rejection of idealism constitutes the basis for the received wisdom about the kind of understandings which inhere in Realism. Realism is seen as deriving from 'a firm belief in a commonly experienced, objectively existing world of history' and as having as its premise 'the materialist, positivist and empiricist

---

9 See, for example, U. Eisele, 'Realismus-Problematik: Überlegungen zur Forschungssituation', *DVjs*, 51 (1977), 163.

10 See R. C. Cowen, *Der poetische Realismus*, (Munich, 1975), p. 22, and J. Rothenburg, *Gottfried Keller. Symbolgehalt und Realitätserfassung seines Erzählens*, (Heidelberg, 1976), pp. 45f.

11 H. Hettner, 'Die romantische Schule in ihrem inneren Zusammenhange mit Göthe und Schiller' in *Realismus und Gründerzeit*, ed. M. Bucher et al, (Stuttgart, 1975), II, 64.

12 B. Auerbach, 'Gottfried Keller von Zürich', ibid, 105.

world-view'. [13] But above all it is seen as having an essentially unproblematic, indeed naive, epistemology and one which has to await modernism and preferably post-modernism for its problematisation. [14] Metafiction, we are told, is a form of fiction which draws attention to itself as fiction and to its status as artifact, which 'exposes the inauthenticity of the realist assumption of a simple extension of the fictive into the real world' and vice versa, and which by virtue of its exposition of that inauthenticity has as its aim the posing of questions about the nature of the relationship between fiction and reality. [15] If it is, on the one hand, the function of realist fiction effectively to naturalise ideology, [16] to present as unproblematic the structures of signs and to imply their unquestionable legitimation within an independent system, above all a system which is independent of linguistic and other codes and which suppresses any suggestion of secondary signification, then it is the function of metafiction to open up that seemingly seamless web. Metafiction ultimately lays bear the very conventions of realism, [17] but what is less clear is whether one can assume a unitary set of aims and effects, specifically for our purposes here it may be essential to draw fundamental distinction between self-reflexivity as it occurs in metafiction in the twentieth century to which the comments above relate, and the function which self-reflexivity may perform in the context of nineteenth-century German fiction. The contention here, but this I stress is provisional, is that a central focus of German self-reflexivity is not status but process, the process whereby meaning is generated, which includes the self-reflexive act itself; [18] the text as statement becomes a meditation on the very conditions and means of its own being, this, however, not in the endless series of inner refractions, but this in the sense of the recognition of the provisionality and relativity of any meaning or statement, where the provisionality and relativity is demonstrably a function of contingency on material circumstance.

What, then, I wish to argue is that German realism may be distinguished from

---

[13] P. Waugh, *Metafiction. The Theory and Practice of Self-Conscious Fiction*, (London, 1984), pp. 6f.

[14] Becker, op. cit., p. 28, is typical of this view.

[15] Waugh, op. cit., pp. 2 and 101.

[16] R. Tallis, *Not Saussure. A Critique of Post-Saussurean Literary Theory*, (Basingstoke, 1988), p. 18, and *Realismus und Gründerzeit*, op. cit., I, 43.

[17] Waugh, op. cit., p. 18.

[18] As such, Realism would be closely related to the development of materialist thought, see D. J. Levy, *Realism. An Essay in Interpretation and Social Reality*, (Manchester, 1981), p. 73.

other European realist traditions by virtue of its self-reflexive attitude. That attitude is not to be seen as an anticipation of instances of twentieth-century self-reflexivity, but rather as a distinct form of self-awareness which recognises the fallacy of autonomous discourse and acknowledges the centrality of system, materially conceived and founded, as the defining context and network within which meaning, identity and so forth are generated. The self-reflexivity is thus directed not towards the ontological status of the text, but rather towards the process whereby the text is constructed, the process of which, of course, self-reflexive discourse is also a part. The real can only be imaginary, but that imaginary is materially constructed and is hence provisional and relative, subject to change, either synchronically or diachronically, within a fixed and determinate and determined range of other possible provisional and relative systems. [19]

To identify this range of issue in certain texts is almost an imperative, since it is to do no more than to explicate and elaborate on the immediate self-understanding that the text is communicating. An obvious example of such a highly foregrounded self-reflexive text would be Storm's *Der Schimmelreiter* where the debate in the first frame and in the second frame both at the beginning and end of the text as well as by virtue of numerous other allusions bears witness to a very immediate concern with the process of narrative itself and an awareness of narrative as a provisional construct communicating but one possible sense, where that sense is shown to be a function of other definable and material conditions. Meaning and truth are shown as categories with no claim to metaphysical status whereby language would function merely as a secondary formation of that status, and for that reason the text then requires of the reader the 'interpretative gamble', [20] while making clear the grounds on, or context within, which that gamble is made. This is not a choice between or amongst different and differing ontologies, rather the reader is made vibrantly aware of what else has to be accepted by way of defining context if a specific reading is to be privileged above the others inherent and latent in the text.

In one sense a dimension of self-reflexivity is equally apparent in Keller's *Romeo und Julia auf dem Dorfe,* indeed the phenomenon of literary allusion has frequently been remarked in Keller's work in general. If, however, a different perspective is adopted on this matter from that of, say, the use of literary reference as parody or social criticism, then it may become possible, for example, to

---

[19] See Kohl, op. cit., p. 81.

[20] M. W. Swales, *The German Novelle*, (Princeton, 1977), p. 44.

accommodate Fontane's objections to the text and to broach the vexed issue of
what appears to be a confusion of styles and a peculiar degree of narrative
uncertainty. Fontane writes of *Romeo und Julia*:

> Hier wird historisch nicht gepudelt, aber der Effekt dieser wundervollen
> Erzählung doch dadurch beeinträchtigt, daß die erste Hälfte ganz in
> Realismus, die zweite Hälfte ganz in Romantizismus steckt; die erste
> Hälfte ist eine das echteste Volksleben bis ins kleinste hinein
> wiedergebende Novelle, die zweite Hälfte ist, wenn nicht ein Märchen, so
> doch durchaus märchenhaft.[21]

The charge, then, is that as a result of stylistic inconsistency which, Fontane
goes on to argue, derives from Keller's lacking contact with the people and hence
his inability to capture the genuine tone of a sixteen-year-old, whereas he can use
memories to do an adequate job with the older farmers, the power of the text is in
some way diminished. Moreover Fontane concludes: 'Eine auf den ersten fünfzig
Seiten realistische Geschichte darf auf den letzten fünfzig nicht romantisch sein.
Dadurch kommt ein Bruch in das Ganze, der stört und verwirrt.'[22] Reservations
and concerns of this kind are relatively frequent visitors in the massive critical
literature that now surrounds this tale. Clifford Bernd, for example, concentrating
on the subject matter making up the plot, asserts that the two halves of the
Novelle, as he identifies them, are irreconcilable.[23] Certainly Marti's idiocy marks
the end of the story of the feud and the beginning of the love story, the cast list or
personnel changes, and the narrative time/narrated time relation changes
dramatically: up until this mid-way point fourteen years, but a mere four days for
the second half. It is equally demonstrably stylistically true that fairytale motifs
now start to abound. Some one hundred years before Bernd Franz Servaes mused
that towards the end of the text 'die verführerischsten poetischen Farben' are piled
up 'mit verschwenderischer Fülle' to obscure the lacking motivation which would
allow the poetically beautiful idea of suicide actually to occur to two young people
who are effectively 'unverschuldete, gesunde Wesen, die den Kampf mit dem
Leben nicht zu scheuen brauchen' and who are positioned in a text whose logic,
he asserts, pushes for them indeed to dare this fight.[24]

---

[21] Th. Fontane, *Sämtliche Werke*, ed. W. Keitel, (Munich, 1962ff.), III.1, 495.

[22] Ibid, 496.

[23] C. A. Bernd, *German Poetic Realism*, (Boston, 1981), p. 41.

[24] F. Servaes in E. Hein, *Gottfried Keller. Romeo und Julia auf dem Dorfe*,
(Munich, 1987), p. 95.

There are many possible responses to the acceptable initial observation of a stylistic difference between the two halves of the Novelle, of which the most obvious, presumably, is that the stylistic disjunction is indicative of the simple theme that the cold world of everyday observed reality and the world of romantic fulfilment in love are incompatible: no accommodation is possible between them and since Sali and Vrenchen are caught between these two worlds, unable ultimately to inhabit either one or the other, but equally unable to inhabit some indeterminate realm inbetween them, there is no choice for them but to escape into death.

But already from the very outset Keller has signalled if not a split, at least an awareness of two different levels of discourse, the relationship of which each to the other is extraordinarily difficult to tie down.[25] The title itself seems relatively straightforward, although the English translation *A Village Romeo and Juliet* tends to privilege what is arguably the subordinate element of the conjunction. In the original German the first element is the Romeo and Juliet story which is then qualified as the village or rural version, which sequence issues the implicit invitation to view what is then to come as an analogue of a world-text which presumably articulates an abiding truth of human experience but which in this case has just been located in a different world. That would appear to be the understanding which Auerbach had of the title and is the source of his objections to it:

> Der Titel dieser Erzählung erscheint mir durchaus unpassend; er octroyirt eine Stimmung ... und versetzt in jene Litteratenlitteratur die nicht vom Leben ausgeht, sondern von der gedruckten Welt und ihren Erinnerungen ...[26]

However the discussion conducted in the first paragraph is characterised by what might be seen as an unresolved tension between these two dimensions of the title.

On the one hand we are informed that it would be an act of vain copying to narrate the story were it not for the fact that it finds legitimation by virtue of its origins in a real event. Because it is grounded in that reality the relevance or truth of the story to which our narrative is so closely related that it could be a copy is itself guaranteed. That is to say that the proof or validity of all the 'Fabeln' on which 'die großen alten Werke gebaut sind' are guaranteed by the incident, the

---

[25] G. Keller, *Romeo und Julia auf dem Dorfe* in *Gottfried Keller. Werke*, (Zurich, 1965), IV, 70 - 149, subsequent references are included in the text.

[26] Auerbach, op. cit., 107.

'wirklicher Vorfall' in the real world, and that, it appears is how Keller himself
saw it, although his comment is curiously undialectical. And it is worth just
recalling in this context Keller's insistence that the story could not be divided into
two parts and that he rearranged the order of the stories in the first volume of *Die
Leute von Seldwyla* in order that *Romeo und Julia* could occupy second position,
all of which betray a conscious concern with his craft that is markedly lacking
when it come to the treatment of the close of the story which seems to border in
indifference. More of that later. He wrote to Weibert on 29 August 1875:

> Den Eingang der Erzählung betreffend, so kann derselbe nicht wohl
> weggelassen werden, da der Titel, der nun nicht mehr zu ändern ist, einige
> Worte erfordert. Namentlich ist mir daran gelegen, zu sagen, daß das
> Hauptmotiv der Geschichte sich wirklich wieder begeben hat, weil nur
> dadurch die ganze Arbeit sich rechtfertigt ... Auf diese Weise ist mein
> Werklein keine Nachahmung. [27]

So far, so good, but at the same time, it would appear, the significance of this
'Vorfall' is guaranteed or legitimated, while acknowledging the 'neues Gewand',
by virtue of its affinity to, or indeed its status as a reduplication of, one of these
few 'Fabeln'. Precisely what is going on in this opening paragraph is an issue on
which a certain amount of critical ink has been spilt, not to any particularly
persuasive effect. There is certainly a chiastic structure operating: 'wirklicher
Vorfall - jede jener Fabeln - die Zahl solcher Fabeln - neues Gewand' which might
imply some kind of reciprocity or mutual dependence. But over and beyond that
there is a further containing frame in the paragraph of 'Geschichte' and 'erzählen'
on the one hand and 'Erscheinung' on the other, which ensures that from the very
outset the text is markedly aware of its own fictionality, that is of its own status as
being in some way determined by its identity as literary discourse and of its
possible range of meaning as being delimited by a specifically invoked intertext,
Shakespeare's *Romeo and Juliet*.

But why this instance of obvious self-reflexivity, or if not why, then at least
what is the effect, which question might lead towards an answer to the why? For
what has to be borne in mind is that that section of the text which most obviously
invokes the Romeo and Juliet story is the second part, the part after Marti's idiocy,
the part of which Fontane said that it 'ganz in Romantizismus steckt', the part
that, in other words, might best be characterised as kitsch, an instance of sickly
sweet sentimentality. The cosmic vista of *Romeo and Juliet* is worth recording,

---

[27] G. Keller, *Gesammelte Briefe*, ed. C. Helbling, (Bern, 1950), III.2, 262.

we are told, by virtue of its appearance 'in neuem Gewande' - 'zwingen alsdann die Hand' -, but those new clothes mean that it has to be presented at the level of trivia. As Gail Hart puts it: 'If Keller has attempted to reproduce tragic love in rustic garb ..., his insistence on a realistic milieu has led him to undermine the mythic or tragic character of the love depicted',[28] and in that sense the old 'Fabeln' do not retain their validity, rather they are qualitatively changed by their external form, or, one might say, context.

But the story itself is aware of precisely that change. After Marti's idiocy, the point at which he loses memory and with that memory identity, all that coinciding with the final loss of the remnants of his land - an interesting conjunction -, both the children are in a sense orphans, their past lives are now finished and they have to establish a new identity and new activity in the future, or they have to find a sphere which can accommodate their childish fantasies of a Biedermeier-like marital bliss, and not insignificantly do they then undertake a kind of wandering or questing during which they come to the little market. The reading of this scene is not easy; on the one hand it might be seen as charmingly naive, while on the other it might be described as depicting a scene of cloying sentimentality, but it is equally clear that what is going on here is the establishing of the new identity which the two seek for themselves, an identity which is not unrelated to the secure and regular world which they will have known in their early childhood, an identity which arguably will determine their refusal to contemplate an existence in the orbit of the Schwarzer Geiger, but above all an identity which has its origins in literary discourse:

> Sie lasen eifrig die Sprüche und nie ist etwas Gereimtes und Gedrucktes schöner befunden und tiefer empfunden worden als diese Pfefferkuchensprüche: sie hielten, was sie lasen, in besonderer Absicht auf sich gemacht, so gut schien es ihnen zu passen. (134)

What they are studying, the narrative informs us, is 'diese süße einfache Liebesliteratur' (134), a literature which for all its ostensible innocence and triviality can hardly be described as neutral for what all centres on is a value cluster relating to domesticity, bourgeois solidity, permanence, commitment, fidelity and so forth. Up until this point in the narrative the two have been playing, acting out parts, pretending to money and a future that are unreal. In short, all would seem rosy:

---

[28] G. Hart, *Readers and their Fictions in the Novels and Novellas of Gottfried Keller*, (Chapel Hill and London, 1989), pp. 75f.

> Als sie aber aus dem Dorfe waren und auf das nächstgelegene zugingen,
> wo Kirchweih war, hing Vrenchen an Salis Arm und flüsterte mit
> zitternden Worten: 'Sali! warum sollen wir uns nicht haben und glücklich
> sein!' 'Ich weiß auch nicht warum!' erwiderte er und heftete seine Augen
> an den milden Herbstsonnenschein ... (132)

It is only later that the crucial statements of limitation come:

> Das Gefühl, in der bürgerlichen Welt nur in einer ganz ehrlichen und
> gewissenfreien Ehe glücklich sein zu können, war in ihm ebenso lebendig
> wie in Vrenchen ... (140)

> 'Diesen sind wir entflohen,' sagte Sali, 'aber wie entfliehen wir uns
> selbst? Wie meiden wir uns?' (144)

Sali's question is indeed a fundamental one to which part of the answer is the kind
of persons they have become by virtue of their upbringing:

> Sali und Vrenchen hatten aber noch die Ehre ihres Hauses gesehen in
> zarten Kinderjahren und erinnerten sich, wie wohlgepflegte Kinderchen
> sie gewesen und daß ihre Väter ausgesehen wie andere Manner, geachetet
> und sicher. (141)

But that basis, I would contend, is but activated, interpellated, reproduced and
reinforced by the 'Liebesliteratur'. Here is an almost classic formulation of the
very process of interpellation whereby an ideology hails its subject and then plays
a central role in constituting that very subject, defining and reinforcing its latent
identity.[29] But more fundamentally what is demonstrated in this section is the way
in which a notion as cherished as that of identity is revealed as no more than an
ideological position whose origins are recorded and whose process of creation can
thus be recorded. What is ultimately of little significance is is the simple fact that a
primary factor in constructing the identity of Sali and Vrenchen is this
'Liebesliteratur', but that does not represent a paradox even in a paper concerning
itself with self-reflexive discourse, for unlike within the twentieth-century

---

[29] See L Althusser, *Lenin and Philosophy and other Essays*, transl. B. Brewster,
(London, 1971), p.160: '... the category of the subject is constitutive of all ideology,
but at the same time and immediately I add that the category of the subject is only
constitutive of all ideology insofar as all ideology has the function (which defines it)
of constituting concrete individuals as subjects'. This kind of understanding is far
removed from the idealist humanistic tradition of which H. W. Fife may be seen as
representative, 'Keller's Dark Fiddler in Nineteenth Century Symbolism of Evil'
*GLL*, 16 (1962/3), 124: 'The young lovers, in rejecting a life of immorality, rise
above adverse circumstances by an act of free will, and though this act destroys
them, it also confirms the power of youth and the influence of society at its best.'

tradition of metafiction, the invocation of metafictional discourse here is not an end in itself, not a demonstration of the text's awareness of itself as fiction, but rather is a metaphor for a demonstration of the process whereby meaning is constructed.

Context, not idealist referent, is the origin of meaning, but since that context is identifiable and consequently transparent to analysis, the consequence must be that any meaning is provisional and relative, provisional within and relative to that context. Change the context and the meaning changes, and hence far from fulfilling the task of naturalising ideology, German realism through metafiction, that is through its self-awareness and self-reflexivity, is demonstrating the process of its own construction and thereby laying bare its own ideological position - something which is not that far away from Fontane's concept of 'Verklärung'. For at the end we are, notoriously, presented with a different context for interpreting the events of the text - a different discourse and with that a different ideology:

> Als man später unterhalb der Stadt die Leichen fand und ihre Herkunft ausgemittelt hatte, war in den Zeitungen zu lesen, zwei junge Leute, die Kinder zweier blutarmen zu Grunde gegangenen Familien, welche in unversöhnlicher Feindschaft lebten, hätten im Wasser den Tod gesucht, nachdem sie einen ganzen Nachmittag herzlich miteinander getanzt und sich belustigt auf einer Kirchweih. Es sei dies Ereignis vermutlich in Verbindung zu bringen mit einem Heuschiff aus jener Gegend, welches ohne Schiffleute in der Stadt gelandet sei, und man nehme an, die jungen Leute haben das Schiff entwendet, um darauf ihre verzweifelte und gottverlassene Hochzeit zu halten, abermals ein Zeichen von der um sich greifenden Entsittlichung und Verwilderung der Leidenschaften. (149)

Originally there was a further section of narrative comment which swithers between some form of approbrium on the one hand, and then an acceptance that the suicide is potentially more moral than the examples of moral laxity that are otherwise to be found nowadays. When it came to publication in 1871 in Heyse's *Deutscher Novellenschatz* Keller asked Heyse to cut the end to what has now become the standard text, or to leave the moral comment, or, if Heyse felt it appropriate, to leave the whole thing as it was. What does this seeming indecision or indifference convey? either precisely indecision and indifference, or alternatively a recognition of the absence of fixed meaning other than in the sense of multi-valency, and hence the irrelevance of adding on, or omitting, further interpretative frameworks. The seemingly cavalier attitude then becomes entirely explicable in that if meaning is relative to context, and any number of different contexts can be adduced, then there can be no definitive conclusions.[30]

Finally, and even more tentatively, a word as to why, once again taking the lead from Keller for the very specific reason that as a leading figure of German realism he is one of the more important figures to have bridged the divide of 1848. His comments to Baumgartner of 28 January 1849 concerning a *tabula rasa* in his religious attitude and the famous letter of 4 March 1851 to Hettner in which he records the irrelevance of the classical period for his own age and the need to strive for new forms within a general acceptance of historical relativity, and lastly by way of summary his observation over ten years later again to Hettner: 'Ich halte dafür, daß es nur darauf ankommt, überall den rechten Faden zu finden, der an die Zeit bindet. Was lebendig ist, ist immer zeitgemäß', these all record a sceptical awareness of status and identity as a writer as well as a fundamental recognition of change and shifting categories.[31] The failure of the liberal idealist position in 1848 with the accompanying wave of depression sets the basis for the acceptance of material determination and with that a specific form of relativism. It is that latter conjunction that is crucial. From at least Brinkmann onwards the phenomenon of both multi-perspectivism and withdrawal into subjectivity have been recognised in the literature of the period,[32] but this should not be seen as a slide into, or a precursor of, neo-Kantian impressionism or indeed neo-Romanticism - it is a multi-perspectivism which knows of its own conditions of being, of its own materiality and provisionality. It is, in other words, self-reflexive for a purpose, and criticism must be careful not to dehistoricise that self-reflexivity thereby rendering it dysfunctional.[33] I quote:

---

[30] What is simply untenable is the position argued by W. Silz, *Realism and Reality*, (Chapel Hill, 1954), p. 80: 'The "Rahmen" in this case is minimal, being restricted to one paragraph at the beginning and one at the end, both really dispensable.'

[31] To Baumgartner, 28.1.1849 in *Gesammelte Briefe*, I, 274; to Hettner, 4.3.1851 and Autumn 1862 in *Gesammelte Briefe*, I, 353f. and 445. The experience of transition is argued by L. B. Jennings, 'The Model of the Self in Gottfried Keller's Prose', *GQ*, 55 (1983), 195, and K. T. Locher. *Gottfried Keller. Welterfahrung, Wertstruktur und Stil*, (Bern, 1985).

[32] R. Brinkmann, *Wirklichkeit und Illusion*, (Tübingen, 2/1966).

[33] Cf. 'Introduction' by W. Q. Boelhower to L. Goldmann, *Method in the Sociology of Literature*, (Oxford, 1981), p.10: 'For Goldmann, structures do not have idealistic or neo-Kantian elements. It is men acting collectively along class lines who create structures and transform them. Nor need one appeal to a metaphysical level to analyze structures. In doing so, one naturally opens oneself to an epistemological dualism, where structures are partly dehistoricized, and, thus, are made partly dysfunctional.'

'The "textual real" is related to the historical real, not as an imaginary transposition of it, but as the product of certain signifying practices whose source and referent is, in the last instance, history itself',[34] but history is, of course 'Geschichte'. In *Der arme Spielmann* Jakob may claim not to have a 'Geschichte', but as he settles down, 'schlug sitzend ein Bein über das andere und nahm überhaupt die Lage eines mit Bequemlichkeit Erzählenden an', and as he speaks he interrupts himself: '"Um diese Zeit - Sieh nur", unterbrach er sich, "es gibt doch eine Art Geschichte. Erzählen wir die Geschichte"',[35] and when the tale has been told, Jakob makes sense as a character, specifically what the narrator has been searching for, a 'Zusammehang', has been established. But it is only one - we see it made, we see it make Jakob, but we know of others, and we know how they are made and we see them make Jakob. What Klaus-Detlef Müller observes of the realists in general is no less true of their literary texts: 'Auffällig ist nämlich das hohe poetologische und ästhetische Reflexionsniveau des deutschen Realismus.'[36]

---

[34] Eagleton, op. cit., p. 75.

[35] F. Grillparzer, *Sämtliche Werke*, ed. P. Frank and K. Pörnbacher, (Munich, 1960ff.), II, 158 and 161.

[36] K.-D. Müller, *Bürgerlicher Realismus. Grundlagen und Interpretationen*, (Königstein/Ts, 1981), p. 11.

# Realism and Moral Design

by Patricia Howe

From its beginnings in Germany the novel is seen as a frivolous foreign form not regulated by poetic norms. Early opponents view it as a challenge to scripture that sets up imaginary, oppositional worlds in order to improve on creation and on the canonical texts which record creation's laws: 'Wer Romans list,' says one, 'der list Lügen.'[1] These imaginary worlds lull their readers into a stupor in which they neither think, act nor even dream for themselves, and entice them from the path of virtue. 'Das schandsüchtige Amadisbuch', for example:

> hat manichen Liebhaber/ auch unter dem Frauenzimer/ deren noch keine dadurch gebessert/ aber wol unterschiedliche zur unziemliche Frecheit angespornet sind...[2]

Its critics particularly regret:

> wie viel das lesen der Liebes=geschichte öffters Unfug angerichtet, und

---

[1] Gotthard Heidegger, *Mythoscopia romantica: oder Discours Von den so benanten Romans*, (Zürich 1698), quoted in: E. Lämmert und H. Eggert, *Romantheorie. Dokumentation ihrer Geschichte in Deutschland 1620-1880*, (Köln, Berlin, 1971), p. 55.

[2] Andreas Heinrich Buchholtz, *Des Christlichen Teutschen Groß=Fürsten Herkules/ Und Der Böhmischen Königlichen Fräulein Valiska Wunder=Geschichte*, (Braunschweig, 1659), p. 1, quoted in Lämmert, p. 13.

wie mancher kerl drüber zum Narren worden, daß er sich beredet, er sey
ein Heros einer Liebes=Geschichte; wie mancher Frauenzimmer gemeinet,
es wären in dem Ehestande lauter solche Süßigkeiten anzutreffen, als in
denen *Romans* beschrieben werden ...[3]

Their answer to the problem becomes an abiding literary precept for the next two
centuries: 'Wer mit seinem Buch erbauen will/ der muß die Laster bestrafft/ und
die Tugend belohnt beschreiben.'[4]

To see the novel as such a challenge is to consider the world of fiction as
ontologically equal to the everyday world and to believe in the capacity of fiction
to permeate and interfere with that world.[5] It is to recognise the novel as
oppositional discourse, calling society and its approved institutions into question.
Such beliefs lurk behind every subsequent debate on the German novel and every
phase of its development. The result is a struggle for a legitimate form and
function, for example, by incorporation into authoritative texts, by a deepening of
thematic concerns and their formal expression, or by transformation into a
compendium of poetic and philosophical forms. In the nineteenth century a salient
feature of the novel's pursuit of respectability lies in recuperating an everyday
world, but a world that testifies to a grand moral design in which all human lives
participate.

Although we cannot say with certainty whether the nineteenth century
constructs this model of reality from conviction or from a sense that reality in its
diversity is becoming an elusive concept, the literature of the age reflects it. In his
study of Victorian conventions John R Reed contrasts the modern view that
'circumstantial authenticity is a conclusive test of realism' with the Victorian belief
that realistic writing must also make the moral design of the world transparent.[6]
Thus the literature of the age shows realism, in the sense of the faithful depiction
of objects and events, going hand in hand with idealism, with the desire to uphold
moral precepts and to inspire the reader with a desire for what is good. Popular

---

[3] Christian Thomas, *Schertz= und Ernsthaffter, Vernünfftiger und Einfältiger
Gedancken/ über allerhand Lustige und nützliche Bücher und Fragen Erster
Monath oder Januarius*, (Frankfurt, Leipzig, 1688), quoted in Lämmert, p. 43.

[4] Siegmund von Birken, *Teutsche Rede-bind und Dicht-Kunst/ oder Kurze
Anweisung zur Teutschen Poesy*, (Nürnberg, 1679), quoted in Lämmert, p. 27.

[5] For a discussion of the ontological status of fictional worlds, see T. G. Pavel,
*Fictional Worlds*, (Cambridge, Mass., 1986).

[6] J. R. Reed, *Victorian Conventions*, (Ohio University Press, 1975), p.4. I am
indebted to this work for the term 'moral design' and for a general definition of its
meaning for Victorian literature.

German fiction expresses this as a longing for a sense of nationhood, a unified political consciousness. [7] Both carry out their aims through implicit and explicit stylizations, some of them no longer transparent to modern readers, which reflect a 'tendency to conceive of existence in terms of moral structures with foundations of fairy-tale morality'. [8] These aesthetic stylizations translate the moral bases of fairy-tale and of Christian fable into experiential models for a pragmatic, even prosaic age.

Moral design is a decisive, but temporary part of the realist code that German Realism shares with European Realism, not merely in its broad shape but in the individual stylizations it generates. It provides fiction with an authorising idea that corresponds generally to the archetypal pattern of fairy tale, the pattern of order/disorder/order restored. This pattern generates the contrastive tension on which the narrative depends. [9] The insistence of fairy tale narrators on perfectionism creates the congruence of moral theme and aesthetic form. This pattern coincides with a basic narrative form identified by Bakhtin, a sequence 'portraying the whole of an individual's life in its more important moments of *crisis*, ... showing how an individual becomes other than he was ...' [10] Bakhtin stresses that the hero's own moral weakness, error, or in Christian terms, sin, initiates a narrative sequence, leading from guilt through punishment to redemption. He suggests, further, that the public nature of the novel, contradicts the privacy of events and introduces legal-criminal categories as specific forms of uncovering and making private life public. [11] Such narratives thus depend on and exploit a sense of the permeability of the fictional world and the reader's world.

In nineteenth-century realism moral design becomes the counterbalance to redundant detail. Its interest lies not in plenitude or diversity but in the exemplary. In accordance with the realistic code, it favours the typical rather than the singular. But it modifies the random inclusion of figures and events by its insistence on moral causality. This is the aspect of moral design that realistic writers have most

---

[7] G. L. Mosse, 'Was die Deutschen wirklich lasen. Marlitt, May, Ganghofer' in R. Grimm und J. Hermand (eds), *Popularität und Trivialität*, (Munich, 1974), pp.101 - 19.

[8] Reed, op. cit., p. 6.

[9] See M. Lüthi, *The Fairy Tale as Art Form and Portrait of Man*, transl. J. Erickson, (Bloomington, 1984), pp. 54 - 7.

[10] M. M. Bakhtin, 'Forms of Time and the Chronotope in the Novel' in *The Dialogic Imagination*, ed. M. Holquist, (Austin, 1981), p. 115.

[11] Ibid, p.124.

difficulty in accommodating, - unlike those seventeenth century critics who see it as a means to legitimise the novel. For the moral design generates 'artistic or compositional' structures, that is, structures in which events are motivated by the need to fit a preconceived pattern, rather than allowed to emerge as the natural outcome of earlier events. [12]

Moral design entails other constraints. It conflates beauty and morality as it 'becomes a consciously controlled esthetic event, patterned upon, though not stipulated by, a sacred model'.[13] It compels the narrator to assume a moral and narrative position above and outside his or her creation and to use a linguistic register compatible with his or her moral and social function; for the author is identified with the narrator, and endowed by the reading public with moral as well as literary authority. Thus it not only restricts circumstantial authenticity, but also discourages linguistic diversity. For the controlling impulse of moral design is at odds with the ability of language to escape into other discourses and so to introduce heterogeneous worlds, at least implicitly or tangentially, into what is intended to be a homogeneous world.

While popular fiction preserves the traditional moral design readily, serious writers question the possibility of combining opposing narrative codes. In their works the congruence of moral and aesthetic conventions fails and the stylizations of realism mutate. I should like here to consider some of these stylizations as they break down in the last decade of the nineteenth century, concentrating on Fontane's *Effi Briest* (1895), but also mentioning Ebner-Eschenbach's *Unsühnbar* (1890) and Saar's *Schloß Kostenitz* (1892). With their central motif of real or imaginary infidelity punished, these narratives express the most common form of moral design, 'the movement ... from an uninformed and sometimes pleasing condition, through redemptive struggle and suffering, to joy or resignation'.[14]

Fontane's familiarity with writers like Dickens gives him access to the Victorian convention of moral design and its stylizations. His view of the basic moral pattern undergoes a shift from confident belief in guilt and punishment as

---

[12] The distinction between artistic and compositional motivation and realistic motivation to describe events reuired for a traditional pattern as opposed to events that are the outcome of earlier events, is made by B. Tomashevsky, 'Thematics', (1925), in *Russian Formalist Criticism: Four Essays*, ed. L. Lemon and M. Reis, (Lincoln, Nebraska, 1965), pp. 61-95; it is discussed in W. Martin, *Recent Theories of Narrative*, (Ithaca and London, 1986), p. 66.

[13] Reed, op. cit., p. 25.

[14] Reed, op. cit., p. 8.

the poles between which a narrative is strung, to sceptical reassessment, a shift
that mirrors that of the age. In 1878, while preparing to write *Schach von
Wuthenow* he writes:

> ... der eigentliche Kern zu einer Novelle kann in vier Zeilen stecken ... es
> kommt immer auf zweierlei an; auf die Charaktere und auf ein
> nachweisbares oder poetisch zu mutmaßendes Verhältnis von Schuld und
> Strafe. Hat man *das*, so findet der, der sein Metier versteht, alles andre
> von selbst. [15]

He anticipates here the simple displacement of the archetypal pattern, but over
the next decade he recognises the difficulties of accommodating this pattern in a
realistic context. In his criticism of other narratives he contrasts the distortions
created by giving prominence to a moral message, with its inherent threat of
dogmatism, with those created by aesthetic licence and its corresponding threat of
chaos. He shows himself as a child of his time when he rejects Smollett's
portrayal of wickedness, describing it as 'wirklich altmodisch', because:

> Die bloße Gemeinheit, ohne alles Erklärende und Versöhnende, wirkt
> einfach häßlich und das bloß Häßliche gehört wohl nicht in die Kunst. [16]

But he also criticises Keller unjustly for being monolingual, for subjecting his
material to too much control, detaching it from its historical and social reference
points and hence from linguistic differentiation:

> Er erzählt nicht aus einem bestimmten Jahrhundert, kaum aus einem
> bestimmten Lande, gewiß nicht aus ständisch gegliederten und deshalb
> sprachlich verschiedenen Verhältnissen heraus, sondern hat für seine
> Darstellungen eine im *wesentlichen sich gleichbleibende Märchensprache*,
> an der alte und neue Zeit, vornehm und gering gleichmässig partizipieren.
> [Fontane's emphasis] [17]

Beyond both the chaos of appearances that he discerns in the novels of Smollett,
Sterne or Zola, and the control of Keller's narrative writing, there are ideological
points of view that Fontane finds untenable. He comes to reject the conflation of

---

[15] Th. Fontane, *Werke, Schriften und Briefe.* ed. W. Keitel & H. Nürnberger,
(Munich, 1962ff.), I, 959. Subsequent references to Fontane's works are taken from
this edition and indicated by volume and page in the text.

[16] Th. Fontane, *Aufsätze, Kritiken, Erinnerungen*, ed. W. Keitel & H.
Nürnberger, (Munich, 1969), I, 895.

[17] Ibid, 494.

the moral and the aesthetic in favour of a relationship that recognises narrative as an act of mediation: 'Realismus ist die künstlerische Wiedergabe (nicht das bloße Abschreiben des Lebens).' [18] He recognises that meaning is generated both in reading and in writing, but that it cannot be imposed: 'Es bleibt bei der bekannten Kinderunterschrift: Dies soll ein Baum sein', and, from the same letter: 'Man muß schon zufrieden sein, wenn wenigstens der Totaleindruck der ist: Ja, das ist Leben.' (II, 920)

When he comes to write *Effi Briest* he goes beyond simple displacement to use the patterns of order and disorder, of fairy tale and other fictions to explore how such meaning is derived. 'Schuld und Strafe' and the stylistic conventions they entail become thematicised; they are formal and referential problems of the narrative. In the course of it their nature and meaning change, and they do so because the world that Effi, Innstetten and the Briests inhabit, is permeated by other fictional and non-fictional discourses. At the beginning the central characters know how guilt is incurred and view retribution as its inevitable consequence, but the code by which they live is itself a jumble of moral, social and aesthetic injunctions. The preparations for Effi's wedding shows this confusion of categories at its most extreme: it is a time when the emotional experience and moral responsibilities of marriage are hopelessly entangled with material acquisition, social advancement and youthful imaginings. What she knows about love, about renunciation, about infidelity, comes from tales whose tellers, unlike Effi herself, can clearly distinguish the canonical from the mythological. For she has not yet grasped that one discourse is paramount in her society, the discourse represented by her mother's social certainties and Innstetten's 'Prinzipienreiterei'. The inability to distinguish ethical, social or aesthetic constraints, mythological and canonical discourses or to apply theoretical knowledge to her own life creates a fragmented sensibility. For example, Effi knows from Pastor Niemeyer about the Byzantine practice of drowning adulterous women, but draws no moral from it for her own life; her affair with Crampas makes her feel guilt but not shame; she ignores her conscience except as it is represented by the picture of the Chinaman. She has a partial sense of the parallels between her relationship with Crampas and that of her servant Roswitha with the coachman, and while she reprimands Roswitha and warns her that sickly wives last longest, she cannot apply Roswitha's experience of losing her child to herself.

Her natural idiom blurs aesthetic and moral categories, for example, when she

---

[18] Ibid, 540.

comments on Crampas' refusal to take his wife to Oberförster Ring's party, although other women will be present: 'Aber dann ist es doch auch häßlich von ihm, ich meine von Crampas, und so was bestraft sich immer' (IV, 147), or when she falls on her knees at the announcement that she and Innstetten are leaving Kessin: 'Sie hatte sich durch ein schönes Gefühl, das nicht viel was andres als ein Bekenntnis ihrer Schuld war, hinreißen lassen und dabei mehr gesagt, als sie sagen durfte' (IV, 182).

She accepts her own guilt only when she and Innstetten are leaving for Berlin, yet her letter to Crampas suggests guilt is not absolute - she allows for mitigating circumstances in his behaviour, and, for herself, links not guilt and punishment, but guilt and forgiveness:

> alle Schuld ist bei mir. Blick' ich auf Ihr Haus ... Ihr Tun mag entschuldbar sein, nicht das meine. Meine Schuld ist sehr schwer. Aber vielleicht kann ich noch heraus. Daß wir hier abberufen wurden, ist mir wie ein Zeichen, daß ich noch zu Gnaden angenommen werden kann. (IV, 190)

The appeal to grace is a way out of the confusion, for it transcends the simple oppositions of order and disorder, and while the idea of grace is part of her rudimentary religious education, it also invokes experience beyond social categories.

Effi's sense of emptiness and of a sensibility split between the harsh certainties of her mother and the slippery arguments of Crampas, has a parallel in Innstetten's shifting attitude to seeking redress. He justifies killing Crampas with the formula: 'Schuld verlangt Sühne'. But this simplistic idea dissolves in his anguished question 'Wo liegt die Grenze? Zehn Jahre verlangen noch ein Duell, und da heißt es Ehre, und nach elf Jahren oder vielleicht schon bei zehneinhalb heißt es Unsinn ... Die Grenze, die Grenze. Wo ist sie? Wo war sie?' (IV, 243) His existential anguish matches Effi's social and physical decline. Both are linked to their respective failure to burn the letters, for this failure brings them up against the irreversible sequence of time that generates meaning in lives and in the discourses that mediate them.

The moral design of the literature of transgression, of novels of adultery or *Kriminalromane*, makes this irreversibility seems to be absolute. The irreversible movement of the narrative sequence is designed to be the bearer of finished meaning. It contrasts with the *Bildungsroman*, likewise an example of Bakhtin's narrative of development, which allows both serious and trivial errors to be made, rectified, repeated, so that, at any stage of the narrative but the ending, they have a provisional meaning that is susceptible to revision. Innstetten's question 'Wo liegt die Grenze?', coming just after he has killed Crampas, shows the narrative design in flux. His insistence on the duel underpins the conventional moral design, but this design is predicated on the notion that disorder destroyed will give way to order, and this simple substitution no longer works.

The link between guilt and punishment, and fiction entails another nineteenth-century convention, namely that of disguise. [19] This is inextricably connected to the problem of identity, in which empirical and metaphysical problems coincide. Disguise raises the empirical problem of verifying identity, for which the nineteenth century, for all its fascination with the mysteries of birth and origins, does not yet possess reliable means, so that imposture is not uncommon. [20] But beyond this, as people in the latter part of the century feel increasingly at odds with what traditional society demands of them, they begin to believe that social identity is a mask. Ultimately this may coincide with a general belief that earthly existence is a disguise and that only spiritual identity is true.

In *Effi Briest* Fontane creates a web of motifs and themes - identity, disguise, play-acting, fairy tales, which have a common origin in the interactions of fiction and reality. Effi's identity blurs the distinction between fiction and reality at every level of the narrative; at the simplest level, the novel is called *Effi Briest* but its heroine becomes Baronin von Innstetten in Chapter Five and reclaims her old name only in death. This is first an admission of failure, but it may imply that she saw her marriage as a fiction. From the beginning her marriage is connected with fictions, first with versions of Cinderella, when she proposes to change her childish clothes before meeting Innstetten - 'in fünf Minuten ist Aschenpuddel in eine Prinzessin verwandelt' (IV, 17), when she sees Roderich Bendix' *Aschenbrödel* in Berlin - 'Da hätte sie wirklich selber mitspielen mögen' (IV, 27) -, and then with the scene from *Das Käthchen von Heilbronn* that is performed at her wedding. These fictions suggest her desire for social advancement - 'Und wie reizend im letzten Akt Aschenbrödels Erwachen als Prinzessin oder doch wenigstens als Gräfin' (IV, 27); but Briest's insistence that the Briests are an old family and Innstetten is not 'ein verkappter Hohenzoller' exposes as false the idea

---

[19] For an account of this convention see Reed, op. cit., pp. 289 - 361.

[20] Ibid, p. 291. In discussing this phenomenon Reed refers to the famous case of the Tichborne claimant.

that Effi might be a Cinderella or a Käthchen, and dismisses the rags-to-riches fairy-tales that underpin many nineteenth century novels. In one sense Briest's remarks naturalise the fairy tale, dismissing the fantastic from real life and the realist narrative, but the fairy tale is ultimately re-instated as anti-*Märchen* as Effi's story comes close to reversing Cinderella's.

Effi's role as the aristocratic Ella who desires 'Ein Schritt vom Wege' generates an intertextual exploration of the dependence of one fiction on another. In his review of *Ein Schritt vom Wege* Fontane describes it as an 'Inkognitokomödie', whose heroine has to pretend to be an Italian singer, Signora Carlina, in order to pay hotel bills after her husband loses his papers. She is so successful that, when the real Signora Carlina and her royal escort arrive at the hotel, they are treated as impostors. Ella's successful deception traps her in the role of Italian opera singer. In *Effi Briest* this fiction produces two others: the first is the professional life of the singer, Marietta Trippelli, whom Effi admires and whose talent enables her to disguise herself:

> ... nun ist sie gut deutsch und stammt von Trippel. Ist sie denn so vorzüglich, daß sie wagen konnte, sich so zu italienisieren? (IV, 86)

To Innstetten this deception is dangerous:

> Was dir so verlockend erscheint - und ich rechne auch ein Leben dahin, wie's die Trippelli führt -, das bezahlt man in der Regel mit seinem Glück. (IV, 87)

but he too is enchanted by the perfection of Marietta Trippelli's disguise which gives a kind of authenticity to what is essentially 'Komödie' (IV, 96). The second fiction is more complex: it begins with Effi's playing the part of Ella, which leads her through involvement with Crampas into other fictions, into the deceit that accompanies her affair, the hypocrisy of judging Roswitha and the pretence of feigned illness, which in turn, as her mother warns her, becomes a real one. When she wants to avoid returning from house-hunting in Berlin to Kessin: 'sie mußte wieder eine Komödie spielen, mußte krank werden' (IV, 197). Rummschüttel's private diagnosis takes up the metaphor: 'Schulkrank und mit Virtuosität gespielt. Evastochter comme il faut' (IV, 200). The feigned illness is itself a device whereby nineteenth century women in life and fiction obtained legitimate respite from their domestic roles. Fontane sounds a warning note by linking her fiction to the fictional works she reads during this supposed illness, which include his own favourite *David Copperfield*, which upholds clearly a conventional moral design that rewards the good and punishes the bad.

Innstetten too becomes part of these fictions. Immediately before he reads the fateful letters, he examines the photographs taken of Effi in *Ein Schritt vom Wege* and throughout his debate on justice and revenge he and Wüllersdorf use metaphors of playing and acting: the affair becomes 'Dinge, die sich abgespielt, als Sie noch in Kessin waren' (IV, 234); the decision to involve Wüllersdorf means 'damit war das Spiel aus meiner Hand' (IV, 236). His view that 'Verjährung' is 'etwas Halbes, etwas Schwächliches, zum mindesten was Prosaisches' (IV, 243) again blurs the distinctions between aesthetic and moral categories, and gives the impression that his empty insistence on honour, unsupported by real feelings of hatred or vengeance, is a self-indulgent fantasy. But this fantasy traps him in a cruel fiction:

> Rache ist nichts Schönes, aber was Menschliches und hat ein natürlich menschliches Recht. So aber war alles einer Vorstellung, einem Begriffe zuliebe, war eine gemachte Geschichte, halbe Komödie. Und diese Komödie muß ich nun fortsetzen und muß Effi wegschicken und sie ruinieren und mich mit ... (IV, 243)

There is a sort of narrative fatalism about all this, as fictional roles, assumed imaginatively and for entertainment, entrap them both in dangerously complex but basically false positions. This is possible because, like many people of their time and class, they know only the roles and identities imposed on them by others; these are, most obviously, the role of dependent child and later child-wife, expected to meet adult standards without having an adult's self-determination, and the role of man of honour, unable to think the socially unthinkable. But it is narrative entrapment too. Effi is not the author of the texts that prescribe or inscribe her life. She plays roles written for her, literally and metaphorically. The alternative to her fictional role is significant absence. The text of the novel records neither her consent to the marriage nor to its dissolution, nor any decision to become involved with Crampas. She is absent at the crucial moments of the narrative, when she is divorced, when the duel is fought, most importantly when the letters from Crampas are discovered.

The discovery of the adultery is the point in *Effi Briest* at which the moral design is most prominent and the narrative most susceptible to the charge of compositional rather than realistic construction. In one sense the discovery of the letters is the sort of mechanical device that belongs to compositional structure, but Fontane makes it psychologically plausible by generating a sense of fatalism. Effi is convinced that her guilt will come out - 'Es kommt doch am Ende noch an den Tag' (IV, 219), she says; this makes the musings of the worldly Sophie Zwicker about Effi's failure to burn the letters an irrelevance. It is equally irrelevant for Innstetten to regret that he did not burn them or to suggest that, if Effi is worried about Johanna having the picture of the Chinaman in her purse, she should tell her to burn it. The unburnt letters are merely an outward and visible sign of her inner lack of grace.

The effect for realism is a shift from the metonymic to the metaphorical. The contingent object, like the letters or the picture of the Chinaman, is only superficially instrumental in deciding the outcome of events. It is more significant as a symbolic manifestation of feelings, which would lead to the same outcome. Similarly, in the simple Victorian scheme of things characters disguise themselves literally, assuming an identity contingent on their own: in *East Lynne*, Isabel Vane, the unfaithful wife, returns to her old home as Madame Vine, governess to her own children. Lady Dedlock in *Bleak House* assumes the disguise of a servant. This can be seen as a metonymic exchange of identities, the assumption of a contingent identity that expresses moral failure as social decline. Effi rejects contingent identities, and adopts instead metaphorical identities from fictions that turn her own life into a fiction.

The identities she rejects show her to be a confused child of the dominant Prussian culture of the age of Bismarck, and this in turn shows the simple moral scheme to be entwined with the discourses of politics and scientific determinism. Effi rejects the models of the past offered by her mother or the elderly Frau von Padden, who wants to divert her from her palpable interest in Crampas by sending her Luther's *Tischreden.* One can see her infidelity as a rejection of the identity imposed on her by her mother's wish to marry Innstetten at least vicariously. The birth of Effi's daughter on the anniversary of a Prussian victory and the patriotic speeches at the child's baptism, suggest that this marriage is also made for Prussia. Effi's infidelity with Crampas, 'ein halber Pole', is thus also a rejection and betrayal of the dominant culture. But she also rejects those contingent identities that occupy the other side of the cultural and social divide. She ignores the warnings of or about minor characters like Roswitha and Maria Trippelli because the fates of the Catholic servant and the Italianised singer seem as remote from her own life as those of the distant Byzantine adulteresses. In this she can be seen to assert the dominant culture, to be as Prussian as Innstetten and as capable of turning other lives into 'ciphers for alternative versions of social existence'.[21] It is only in their weakness that Effi and Innstetten contemplate crossing social and cultural boundaries, that they recognise the worth of simpler lives, the lives of animals, of servants, or of distant civilisations.

At this point I should like to bring in the other texts I mentioned earlier, Ebner-Eschenbach's *Unsühnbar* and Saar's *Schloß Kostenitz*. Ebner-Eschenbach and Saar write against a somewhat different literary and political background, but their use of this basic pattern is similar. *Unsühnbar* and *Schloß Kostenitz* show the disjunctions of the age through heroines whose highly developed, individual moral consciences are out of step with contemporary thought and manners. These individual consciences ensure that the pattern of order/disorder/order is carried through in the traditional way, but at the same time re-examined. Ebner-Eschenbach and Saar simplify their task by locating moral judgment in the consciousness of their heroines, who are not found out but confess and judge themselves. Both make an uncompromising judgment, at odds with a society that accepts the appearance for the essence and with a church that offers absolution. Both believe in the moral imperative, but the narrative suggests that they are also at the mercy of a natural force greater than themselves. The juxtaposition of moral absolutism and uncontrollable instincts takes the narratives into the deterministic debate.

In *Unsühnbar* the account of Maria Dornach's fateful encounter with her lover, Tessin, describes them as 'zwei trunkene Menschen' unconscious of honour, duty or fidelity. She is 'unwiderstehlich hingerissen wie von einer Naturgewalt' - and, as Kenworthy notes, the concessive 'wie' is crucial.[22] In support of this view of Maria as helpless in the face of passion, - and she is the only one of these three heroines who loves her seducer passionately - , he cites Ebner-Eschenbach's aphorism: 'Wer an die Freiheit des menschlichen Willens glaubt, hat nie geliebt und nie gehaßt.'[23] Maria's moral absolutism is contrasted with her father's infidelity. This infidelity is an open secret, tolerated according to

---

[21] R. A. Berman, *The Rise of the Modern German Novel*, (Cambridge, Mass. and London, 1986), p. 3.

[22] Marie von Ebner-Eschenbach, *Unsühnbar*, ed. B. Bittrich, in Marie von Ebner-Eschenbach, *Kritische Texte und Deutungen*, ed. K. K. Polheim, (Bonn, 1978), I, 64. Subsequent references to this novel are taken from this edition and appear in the text. B. J. Kenworthy, 'Ethical Realism: Marie von Ebner-Eschenbach's *Unsühnbar*', *GLL*, 41 (1978), 485.

[23] Ibid, 485.

the moral relativism that makes what is beautiful acceptable: 'So ein Herr wie unser Graf, so eine Schönheit, kann der was dafür, daß ihm die Weiber nachlaufen? - s'ist ihre Sach und ihre Schuld' (*Unsühnbar*, 37).

The fruit of this infidelity is Maria's half brother, a rejected, degenerate creature, close to death, who makes himself known as she is about to marry. It is her own infidelity that makes her acknowledge a connection with him. Maria's deep feelings of guilt after this infidelity are first a private agony and then a public act. She rejects suicide, because it means killing her unborn child: this is presented as a religious and a biological imperative:

> Wohl lohte es in ihr auf: Begrabe die Frucht des Frevels mit dir! ... Aber töten, um zu sühnen? - Noch war sie fromm und gläubig und fragte in ihrer Seelenqual: 'Wie würdest du die Kindesmörderin empfangen, ewiger Richter, Herr, mein Gott?'
> Der mächtigste Instinkt im Weibe erhob seine gewaltige Stimme ... Vielleicht auch rang der nun verdoppelte Lebenstrieb - ihr unbewußt - gegen die Vernichtung. (*Unsühnbar*, 71)

She considers confessing her infidelity to her husband, but knows that he will not repudiate her, so that, to her burden of guilt and desire for penitence, she will add the burden of perpetual gratitude. This leave her no choice but play-acting and the private torment of living a lie:

> Maria spielte eine jammervolle Komödie, heuchelte Interesse an gleichgültigen Dingen ... Sie ... grübelte sich allmählich in eine eigentümliche Sophistik hinein. Die Sühne, nach der sie rief, lag gewiß in der Einsicht, das es ihr verwehrt sei, zu sühnen. Der verdammende Schicksalsschluß, der über sie gefällt war, lautete: 'Du liebst die Wahrheit, wandle in der Lüge'. (*Unsühnbar*, 72)

Maria condemns herself to social judgement by confessing her own infidelity after her husband's death, because she cannot perpetuate the wrong she has done and allow her young son by her lover to inherit a title and position that are not rightfully his. This is essentially a moral judgement, since, according to the prevailing law, any child born during her marriage is legally her husband's child. Her inability to accept forgiveness is a personal attribute, for the narrator suggests that this severe judgement goes beyond the demands of religion or society. There is no expiation to be found in social ostracism, for society refuses to reject Maria after her confession of guilt. In her public and private behaviour Maria has seemed too good to be guilty: her husband's cousin excuses her behaviour 'Wo die gesündigt hat, da wäre ein Engel gefallen' (*Unsühnbar*, 122); socially and politically, 'ein Kind der neuen Zeit', she has made herself beloved by being too aware of her privileges to demand them as rights. The title is ultimately problematic, for Maria is guilty of a failing that only she sees a need to expiate, and which can therefore only be removed by death, a death that follows the unwelcome return of her lover and her rejection of him.

*Schloß Kostenitz* creates a disjunction between guilt and expiation by relativising it. It does this twice: first, by reducing the infidelity to a fleeting kiss, which gains such magnitude in the mind of the heroine that she hides from the world and goes into a decline; secondly, by putting this incident and its consequences into a broad historical background, in which it becomes a single episode in the history of a castle and a family. Klothilde, the young wife of an elderly husband, is like Effi, a creature of conflicting impulses, and like Maria, one of uncompromising moral judgements. She is the victim of both her moral absolutism and her unacknowledged sexuality, which shows itself unconsciously in the fear and fascination with which she watches Poiga-Reuhoff, her would-be seducer, breaking in a horse. She has denied her own sexuality; her marriage is childless; her tastes and interests are shallow and belong to a bygone age; her life has become an attempt to remove herself after the 1848 revolution from the dangers of an unstable world, which ended her husband's political career, into the apparently timeless security of Schloß Kostenitz. This retreat from world and time is disrupted by the intrusion of Graf Poiga-Reuhoff, who rekindles the sexuality she has repressed. Although she flees from him after a single kiss, Klothilde punishes herself as thoroughly as Maria Dornach. She confesses to her husband, shuts herself away in the dark and eventually dies. Like Innstetten, her husband reflects on what is to be done. He rejects the idea of a duel as ridiculous and asks the count to leave, but it appears that the regiment has already been called away. He is struck, like Innstetten, by the cruel impossibility of reversing time - if the regiment had been recalled a day earlier, Klothilde would have been spared and their illusion of happy seclusion might have been preserved. Although he does not challenge his wife's would-be seducer, their lives and deaths remain entwined, for he dies immediately after reading of the death of Poiga-Reuhoff in battle.

This individual tragedy occupies a central position in a broader history of the castle of Kostenitz, which stretches backwards and forwards into worlds in which Günthersheim and Klothilde have no share. This broader scheme questions the insistence of individuals on upholding a rigid moral order. But Saar allows for a number of explanations of Klothilde's exaggerated behaviour. In the text the connection between her inflamed feelings and the 'Gehirnentzündung' that kills her is made transparent. Her insistence on punishing herself for a trivial incident clearly suggests that she knows herself capable of much worse, and cannot deal with her conflicting feelings except by destroying them and herself. This may be interpreted as an old-fashioned conflict between passion and virtue, which is her view of it, or as hypersensitivity bordering on the neurotic.

The most tragic aspect of their entrapment in rigid moral and social structures, and the roles these impose, is that the central characters in all these works never know of each other's struggles for a meaningful identity. Each debates and tries to solve a problem in isolation. The isolation of partners from each other produces one of the main formal digressions from the simple moral scheme that we find in late nineteenth century texts, namely the problematic ending. The simple moral design requires a form of resolution in which the fates and emotions of the faithless wife, the wicked seducer and the wronged husband match and so produce a perfect fit between moral and aesthetic design. She must be penitent, her lover must be destroyed, the husband must regain his honour.

Fontane creates an ironic allusion to this in an exchange between the servants, Roswitha and Johanna, when they read about the duel between Innstetten and Crampas in a newspaper. Roswitha expresses sorrow for Effi: 'Und das lesen die Menschen und verschimpfieren mir meine liebe, arme Frau. Und der arme Major. Nun ist er tot.' To which Johanna replies: 'Ja, Roswitha, was denken Sie sich eigentlich. Soll er nicht tot sein? Oder soll unser gnädiger Herr tot sein?' (IV, 246) Johanna's response expresses the controlling and controlled meaning of moral design, the congruence of narrated events and socially sanctioned moral views. Roswitha's appeal to compassion and common humanity belongs to a different discourse that interferes with and disrupts this design.

In the typically moral design of a popular novel like *East Lynne*, the moral responses of the characters to their tragedy dovetail in a way that overcomes their individual pain and accommodates it into the great design which they all acknowledge. The faithless wife dies more mysteriously than Effi, Maria or Klothilde, all of whom are provided with a plausible illness: 'She had no decided disorder, yet Death had marked her', and this unexplained death is accepted by the Victorian reader as necessary for the restoration of order.[24] On her death-bed scene she confesses her guilt to her husband and asks his forgiveness, which he

---

[24] Mrs. Henry Wood, *East Lynne*, (London, 1888), p.446.

grants but not before telling her how wrongly she has behaved. Her death frees
the husband, who had believed her dead, to live a happy and respectable life with
his second wife and family. The second wife, learning of her predecessor's
demise, confesses to fear of not loving her step-children and the work closes with
a moralising exhortation:

> 'Every good thing will come with time that we earnestly seek,' said Mr.
> Carlyle. 'Oh Barbara, never forget - never forget that the only way to
> ensure peace in the end, is to strive always to be doing right, unselfishly,
> under God.'[25]

Fine words, indeed, from a man whom death has just released from bigamy.

*Effi Briest, Unsühnbar* and *Schloß Kostenitz* refuse endings in which the
responses of the characters are so harmonious. Their heroines die, but this is not
completion, for the presence of mixed discourses, aesthetic, moral, psychological
and deterministic, detaches the problem from the outcome. Thus Klothilde may
die from a surfeit of guilt, but then again she may die from a brain haemorrhage or
from a psychosomatic illness. Saar's readers and critics have found the motivation
problematic.[26] Likewise Effi Briest dies apparently of exposure to the cold night
air and Maria Dornach dies of 'Herzruptur'. Neither their deaths nor those of their
would-be seducers restore order, but signal its dissolution. Perhaps most
significantly, the wronged husbands show responses that break with the
traditional moral design. Innstetten feels an existential *angst* that is far beyond the
loss felt by a wronged husband; Günthersheim rejects the idea of a duel because
he can recognise the feelings of the would-be seducer. The death of Maria's
husband precipitates her confession of guilt. There is also a formal disjunction
between ending, in this referential sense, and closure. *Unsühnbar* closes with a
disjunction between Maria's inability to accept forgiveness and a strange
transfiguration; *Schloß Kostenitz* with a jarring contrast between the old and new
lives of the castle and with a speculation, and *Effi Briest* with an injunction
against further questioning.

A final indication of the shifting patterns of the narrative is the diverting of
inheritances, the saving mechanism of such novels as *Felix Holt* and *Jane Eyre*,
where inheritance creates the possibility of a new paradise. The childless hero of
*Schloß Kostenitz* leaves his castle to the community rather than to his relatives,

[25] Ibid, p. 471.

[26] For a discussion of this see E. M .V. Plater, 'Ferdinand von Saar's Schloß
Kostenitz', *Modern Austrian Literature*, 16/2 (1983), 19-33.

with the order that it remain uninhabited for twenty five years after his death. Maria's surviving child, Erich, the son of her lover, is deprived by her confession of his inheritance. Annie Innstetten von der Briest, is scarred by the misery of her parents' lives. Other children are seen skipping in the sunshine by Innstetten.

All convention is an appeal to limits.[27] For writers at the end of the nineteenth century the stylistic conventions and the moral and social scheme they underpin have reached their limits. The narrative dissolves something of its own solidity by revealing the disjunction between morality and feeling and the instability of identity, and by refusing closure. By the end of the century writers recognise that moral design is an aspect of controlled meaning and that neither absolute fidelity to life in all its diversity, nor the stylisations imposed by a particular, predominantly moral view of the world, can be sustained. The next generation reverses or subverts the stylizations and conventions of their predecessors relentlessly, and these, in retrospect, seem to flatten out, to merge and to become indistinguishable from one another, to seem, in short, old-fashioned and irrelevant.

Two examples may suffice: in *Buddenbrooks* (1901) moral design is relativised by juxtaposition with other discourses; we can see this in two consecutive episodes, in the episode in which Thomas Buddenbrook breaks his own and his family's code of business ethics and practice to speculate on a crop not yet harvested, only for it to be ruined by a bit of hail, and in the following discussion about morality and art. The first mimics the traditional pattern - Thomas commits what his ancestors and he, in his heart of hearts, believe to be a sin, and he is punished, but punishment is a relief because it validates the simple, absolute oppositions of the traditional moral scheme. But, in the succeeding discussion on morality and art, Gerda's view that morality is that which is at any given moment opposed to hedonism, combines with the music-master's view that counterpoint, not harmony, promotes development, to suggest that opposition is provisional, relative, even creative. In Heinrich Mann's *Der Untertan* (1918), the pattern of thought that links crime, punishment and fiction is satirised. As a child, Diederich Heßling inhabits a world of both real and fictional horrors, such as 'den Märchenkröten, dem Vater, dem lieben Gott, dem Burggespenst und der Polizei'.[28] In this undifferentiated chaos of fiction and reality, order depends on his childish lies being detected and punished by his father, who ascribes these to

---

[27] For a discussion of this see Pavel, op. cit., pp. 115 - 35.

[28] H. Mann, *Der Untertan*, (Munich, 1964), p.7.

his wife's indulgence and dishonesty, which comes from reading novels: 'Sie verdarb das Kind fürs Leben. Übrigens ertappte er sie geradeso auf Lügen wie den Diedel. Kein Wunder, da sie Romane las!'[29] Not only are we back with the view that 'Wer Romans list/ der list Lügen', but with a novel in which the central character goes on to fictionalise his own world repeatedly, until his fictions shape his life and his life shapes his fictions.

Yet both *Buddenbrooks* and *Der Untertan* depend essentially on the same construction of divisions as *Effi Briest, Unsühnbar* and *Schloß Kostenitz*. The creation of 'ciphers for alternative modes of social existence' and the assertion that one mode is superior to the rest remain prerequisites for asking, for example, what it means to be a Buddenbrook or a loyal subject of the Emperor.

What we witness in the controlled and controlling discourse of moral design has been described as 'ontological focalization'.[30] It is an ordering of possible models of the world, that seems to originate in a need for stability:

> The most conspicuous world model may then play the role of the absolute norm, of a high court that summons neighbouring models for control and justification. In communities that adopt a central model, while still keeping other peripheral landscapes, the chosen model would serve as ultimate truth and regulating principle for the remaining versions: therefore, in case of conflict, the peripheral models have to yield ... If ... orthodoxy imposes a dominant model, it is in order to protect a certain ontological focalisation, a certain ordering of coexistent landscapes. For, observing the large number of beliefs and heresies condemned in the name of one set of convictions or another, one cannot avoid the impression that world models are in a continuous state of fermentation, change, and degradation, in a permanent movement against which the dogmatic reinforcement of a certain order may be the best defence.[31]

Something like this happens in the nineteenth century as it struggles to comes to terms with rapid and radical change. It uses literature to strengthen moral sensibilities and protect threatened ideals, and to provide a framework within which the new may be accommodated. But these functions lose their appeal as authors resist the temptation to treat their readers as children whom they must instruct, or come to see themselves reduced by moral schemes to childishness. When they redraw the traditional patterns, they engage with the conflict between what Bakhtin calls authoritative discourse, which 'binds us, quite independent of

---

[29] Ibid, p. 6.

[30] Pavel, op. cit., p. 139.

[31] Ibid, pp. 139f.

any power it might have to persuade us internally', and internally persuasive discourse, which is 'backed up by no authority at all, and is frequently not even acknowledged in society'.[32] The result is a mingling of narrative codes which 'joins the stylised world with the world of contemporary consciousness', and thus shows how and where these different discourses and the views they articulate collide.[33] On the one hand authoritative discourse ensures that received ideas of morality prevail - infidelity is always discovered, wronged husbands survive lovers, and details of the affair are encoded in a language that displaces sexuality in favour of other activities and appetites. They still depend on the traditional moral design, referentially for the insights it offers into the worlds mediated by their fictions, and formally for the contrastive tension it generates. On the other hand, they recognise increasingly that on both formal and referential levels undifferentiated moral oppositions are inadequate. The recognition that the authoritative language is overcome by being treated as an object leads them to engage with the relationship between fiction and truth through the many fictions in the lives of their characters. They come to the novel, as the hero of Henry James's *The Ambassadors* (1903) comes to Paris:

> primed with a moral scheme of the most approved pattern which was yet framed to break down on any approach to vivid facts; that is to say to any at all liberal appreciation of them.[34]

Their own liberal appreciation and what James calls 'blest imagination' compel them, as they compel James' hero, to submit to a 'drama of discrimination', which eventually reveals the fine graduations contained within the simple oppositions of the approved pattern.

---

[32] Bakhtin, 'Discourse in the Novel' in *The Dialogic Imagination*, op. cit., p. 342.

[33] Ibid, p. 363.

[34] Henry James, *The Ambassadors*, (Oxford, 1985), Preface, p.xxxvii.

# The Reluctant Realist:

# Stifter and his *Bunte Steine*

by Martin Bott

In the wake of Martin Swales' discussion of the topic in 'Neglecting the Weight of the Elephant ...',[1] it is gradually becoming accepted that, in order to do it justice, investigations of German prose fiction require a working definition of 'Realism' which goes beyond simple mimesis. Mark Ward has developed the theme (and that of elephants!) in 'Only an Elephant Can Bear an Elephant's Burden ...',[2] with special reference to the period of so-called Poetic Realism. That Realism is concerned with the individual in the context of his society, that in Realist texts the laws of society to some extent replace an orthodox idealist value system, is relatively uncontroversial. However, in an effort to define the Realism of the last century in Germany more precisely, and thus to free it of unflattering and irrelevant comparisons with the Realism of the same period in the rest of Europe, Ward goes considerably further. He argues that writers such as Fontane reject the

---

[1] M. Swales, '"Negelecting the Weight of the Elephant ...": German Prose Fiction and European Realism', *MLR*, 83 (1988), 882 - 94.

[2] M. G. Ward, '"Only an Elephant can bear an Elephant's Burden": German Realism - The Limits and Limitations of Liberal Reading', *NGS*, 16 (1990/91), 71 - 92.

Western liberal concept of the 'individual' altogether. Their radicalism lies in the fact that their 'characters' cannot engage in conflict with society, only function within it or perish: they are simply the 'intersecting point of materially produced social forces'.[3] The apostrophizing of conventional literary terms such as 'character', 'personality' and even 'individual' is indicative of a problem which he points out himself: that even if we accept that the Realists do achieve the presentation of such a revolutionary perception of the status of human existence, the modern critic is likely to undo that achievement in any examination of such a text, simply because the language he has at his disposal is the language of liberal Western tradition, in which the concepts which are being dismantled by Fontane or Storm are virtually essential elements.

One might quibble that the simple fact of individual differentiation is rather overlooked in this synopsis of the argument, and that it fails to address the fact that even though Effi Briest, for example, perishes because she cannot integrate herself into society, she has nevertheless existed before perishing. Briefly, however doomed she may be, she therefore constitutes an individual who is in a state of opposition to society. Opposition presupposes two sides, so that the concept of the individual as an independent entity is actually postulated, even if it is given no hope of survival. This is more than a mere symptom of the limitations of the language at Fontane's disposal. In fact, of course, it hardly detracts from the implications of Ward's argument, for an individual who is destined to fail is not an individual who in any way threatens the supremacy of society as the only available context for existence and is in fact merely illustrative of it. Ward's discussion of the novel in terms of an inversion of the formula of the 'Bildungsroman' is also important here. Fontane does not offer his child, Effi, the possibility of conventional personal development, merely of social integration or death. The close of the novel sees her virtually reliving her childhood: she has failed to emerge from it and fades away. In this respect we have another index of the radicalism of Fontane's vision: the process of growing up is seen as a process of growing into society; failure to do so is thus a denial even of human identity.

It is an important argument in that it does indeed seem to create a legitimate means of defining German Realism very precisely, recognising and accounting for the fact that the literature of the nineteenth century was indisputably 'different' from that which came before and after it. Its consequences are immense: it follows from it that a proper appreciation of authors such as Keller, Storm and Fontane

---

[3] Ward, op. cit., 80.

must entail a fundamental revision of one's reading strategy.

Any theory which attempts to define the characteristics of a period or school of literature is likely to be of particular interest, however, when applied to authors whose identification within that school is less than entirely clear. The significance, of course, lies not in the satisfaction of having consigned an author to an artificial and retrospectively conceived category, but in the possibility that applying the theory may produce new insights into that author's work.

Adalbert Stifter is one such author. His position in relation to Realism has long been a disputed one: witness the titles of three rather virulent articles which appeared in the fifties: first, 'War Stifter Realist?', then 'Stifter War Realist!' followed by an 'Erwiderung'.[4] Many of the premises of that debate have been superseded, but the issue at stake remains an intriguing one. Let us not be deterred by Lukács' - typically diffident! - description of Stifter as a genuine and legitimate inheritance for the fascists;[5] there is surely more to his work than either Lukács, in his attack on him, or the fascist critics, in their praise, are prepared to admit.

Like his compatriot, Grillparzer, Stifter found himself torn by the events of the 1840s between his liberal inclinations and a deep-seated desire for the stability and order which he saw as being inherent in Habsburg Austria. If their work does exhibit doubts about the relevance of an idealist value system, it is likely to be almost in spite of themselves, and it is this reflection of an inner conflict which perhaps makes both of them so hard to categorize. We shall see that in *Bunte Steine* these inner doubts are clearly discernible, that Stifter constantly tries to soften the impact of a view of human life which matches Fontane's in its radicalism, with the suggestion of a containing, stabilising universal system.

*Turmalin* is perhaps the starkest articulation Stifter ever achieved of his Realist vision. In it he presents us with a chilling picture of the consequences of turning one's back on society. When we re-encounter the Rentherr, midway through the story, his existence is a complete rejection of the idea of social function. He has descended below street level, into a basement flat which he seals up with a paranoia reminiscent of the *Hagestolz*. When our narrator's friend meets him for the first time she is struck by his refined language: it does not fit his role as porter.

---

4 E. Zenker, 'War Stifter Realist?', *Neue deutsche Literatur*, 4 (October 1956), 97 - 109; H. H. Reuter, 'Stifter war Realist!', *NDL*, 5 (September 1957), 120 - 29; E. Zenker, 'Erwiderung', *NDL*, 5 (September 1957), 129 - 36.

5 G. Lukács, 'Der historische Roman' in G. L., *Werke*, (Neuwied, 1962ff.). VI, 301.

In fact, of course, this is not a role which he fulfils at all: he is not paid for it, and Professor Andorf is not even aware that the the building he lives in has a porter. Later, the Rentherr's daughter also surprises the woman by her elevated language, but it is not functional: 'Das Mädchen antwortete mir zu meinem Erstaunen in der reinsten Schriftsprache, aber was es sagte, war kaum zu verstehen.' [6]

Swales and Swales[7] point out that there is a dark element in the story which is represented both in the jerky, eliptical structure of the text itself and in the form of various motifs: the actor Dall, who can flit between sections of society just as he can between his stage roles; the weird 'music' which the Rentherr produces on his flute, so reminiscent of that produced by Jakob, 'Der arme Spielmann' of Grillparzer's text, on his violin; the figures of the Rentherr and his daughter themselves, who remain shrouded in mystery even at the close of the tale. All these represent the exceptional in terms of normal society, and all arouse fascination in the members of that normal society. This fascination is illustrated by the fact that, well meaning as she may be, the woman's behaviour is motivated largely by curiosity, a fact which Stifter (displaying an unexpectedly light touch with irony!) allows to shine delightfully through her own narration. It is not restricted to the 'Bürgertum' (cf. Swales & Swales, p. 182): it is apparent also in the crowd which gathers outside the Perronsche Haus on the death of the Rentherr, which the woman feels it beneath her dignity to approach, and in her concern about the possible reaction of her domestic servants to the girl's deformity.

Intriguing as it may be, this world of 'das Unbegreifliche'[8] is nevertheless portrayed in almost entirely negative terms. The Rentherr has quite plainly failed as a human being: he has lost the sense of proportion which is engendered by social integration and lives entirely in the shadow of his emotional reaction to his wife's disappearance. His condition is that described in the opening paragraph of the story: 'der Mensch, wenn er... sich unbedingt der Innigkeit seiner Freuden und Schmerzen hingibt, den Halt verliert ...' (p. 135). The extent of his failure may be measured by his morbid fascination with his own death: 'beschreibe den Augenblick, wenn ich tot auf der Bahre liegen werde und wenn sie mich begraben' (p. 173) and by the legacy he leaves behind: a deformed, helpless

---

[6] Adalbert Stifter, *Werke und Briefe*, ed. A. Doppler and W. Frühwald, (Stuttgart, 1978ff.), II/2, 164. Subsequent page references are included in the text.

[7] M. & E. Swales, *Adalbert Stifter. A Critical Study*, (Cambridge, 1984), pp. 173 - 83.

[8] Ibid, p. 176.

daughter. Both illustrate clearly that such an existence is not sustainable.

In *Der arme Spielmann*, although the world of the Spielmann initially seems 'unbegreiflich', Grillparzer goes on, through Jakob's own narration, to create a context within which his life can be seen to be reasonable, even if the manner of his death renders it pathetic. It is a life based on premises different from those of the society around him and hence utterly incomprehensible to that society. In *Turmalin*, however, we are given no such context; our internal narrator is locked firmly into the 'bürgerliche' world, and the world of the Rentherr and his daughter remains opaque and disturbing.

Much more clearly than in *Der arme Spielmann*, because Stifter refuses us an illuminating context, succumbing to 'das Unbegreifliche', leading an asocial existence, is seen not as an alternative, but as the terrible consequence of failure, not just in terms of one's social role, but - as in Fontane - in terms of one's human identity. The descent to the basement is in fact a descent from the level of humanity. The daughter's only contact with society is her view of people's legs, and the effects on her of such seclusion are illustrated grotesquely by her swollen head: even her human appearance is distorted. She is more comfortable with her jackdaw than she is with human company; she is so far removed from the premises of normal society that even the word 'death', though she uses it, has no resonance inside her - or at least none which relates to its conventional meaning: 'Als wir in die unterirdische Stube gekommen waren, fragte es nach dem Vater. Ich war in Verlegenheit; denn ich hatte gedeutet, daß es wisse, daß der Vater tot sei; denn es hatte selbst das Wort gebraucht' (p. 170). Similarly, the word 'music' she understands only in terms of the context of the basement, calling it 'Flötenspiel'. It is no coincidence that the Rentherr and his daughter live in the basement of a decaying house, a house in which humanity is gradually retreating before the advance of the animal world. Professor Andorf, himself a cheerful, *sociable* man, has chosen to live there explicitly because 'es seinen dichtenden Kräften, die sich nicht sowohl im Hervorbringen, als vielmehr im Empfangen äußerten, zusagte, das allmähliche Versinken, Vergehen, Verkommen zu beobachten und zu betrachten, wie die Vögel und andere Tiere nach und nach von dem Mauerwerke Besitz nahmen, aus dem sich die Menschen zurückgezogen hatten' (p. 155).

The truly radical aspect of *Turmalin* is that in it, social function is thus seen as the sole definition of humanity. Integration is the 'individual's' only insulation against failure and regression into the animal world. In a sense, then, the individual's only chance of survival is to accept that he does not in fact possess 'individuality', only a role in society. The socially integrated characters - the woman and her husband, the crowd in the street - may be attracted by 'das Unbegreifliche', but they are not vulnerable to it in the way that the Rentherr and his wife prove to be at the start of the tale. The attraction is the frisson of excitement which the dangerous, the exceptional affords those who are conscious of their own security. Thus, though the crowd outside the dead Rentherr's door is curious, 'es ging niemand von ihnen durch das rote Pförtchen hinein, entweder aus Achtung vor dem Toten, der im Innern lag, oder aus Scheu vor dem seltsamen Perronschen Hause' (p. 162). Only when order and legitimacy arrive in the form of the officials does the crowd try to follow them inside - and the woman (although she neglects to admit it) evidently shares this 'Achtung' or 'Scheu', for she does likewise. Again, while the woman's concern for the daughter may be largely dictated by the allure of the exceptional nature of her circumstances, the concern is actually corrective in nature, and indeed, by the end of the story the daughter has to some extent been 'salvaged': she is a viable member of society and her swollen head has subsided.

In contrast to the practicality and gregariousness of the woman and her husband, the Rentherr's household at the start of the story is presented as being dislocated and inhumane. Eve Mason has pointed out that by virtue of the fact that he does not need to earn a living, the Rentherr is already without an active role in the world; [9] even when he ventures outside the flat, it is to watch rather than participate in the chess games. His indiscriminate obsession with portraits of famous people displays an equally passive and clearly unhealthy concern with the exceptional: we cannot imagine that he himself could ever achieve eminence, simply because he is not prepared sufficiently to engage himself in society. His household is supremely non-functional: everything, even the child, is described in terms of its aesthetic rather than its practical or humane aspect; the kitchen, the flat's only truly functional space, is actually situated outside it. The complete absence of any apparent affection or passion within the family is further indicative of a tendency towards inhumanity.

This state of withdrawal is one which Stifter consistently regards as fatal. Unlike the woman and her husband, the Rentherr and his wife are not insulated by any social identity against 'das Unbegreifliche', and the destruction of their household is therefore, in Stifter's terms, entirely logical. He implies this

---

[9] E. Mason. 'Stifter's *Turmalin* A Reconsideration', *MLR*, 72 (1977), 348 - 58.

inevitability in the shockingly casual manner in which he introduces the beginning of the end: 'Endlich fing Dall ein Liebesverhältnis mit der Frau des Rentherrn an und setzte es eine Weile fort' (p. 142). That the Rentherr's wife should be attracted to the actor Dall, a personification of the exceptional, also makes perfect sense: her husband even comments that 'sie habe an Dall fallen müssen' (p. 143). Later our narrator's friend professes a liking for the theatre, but it is inconceivable that she should ever prejudice her security by falling prey to a figure like Dall; in her life, the theatre fits into conventional social routine. Once deserted by his wife, the Rentherr has lost even the appearance of his role as husband, and his passive, asocial existence is too insubstantial to prevent his succumbing to irrationality and eventually retreating to the basement flat.

Such an interpretation of the story, which integrates the text more than Swales and Swales accept is legitimate, does not, however, leave us with a 'neat moral tale'.[10] Rather it recognises that *Turmalin* in fact denies the very existence of an idealist category of 'morality'. It is not morality which is the difference between survival and disaster, between valid and invalid human life, only the degree to which the characters fulfil their social function. Even religion is seen to operate only in these terms. When the woman interrogates the girl about religious matters, she proves to be able to recite the relevant parts of the catechism, but her expressionless eyes belie her: the words are meaningless to her. She has been to church, but never heard any music there or spoken to anybody: 'Es mußte also höchstens bei stillen Messen gewesen sein.' (p. 174). In other words, church going acquires meaning only because it is normally a social activity; religion itself is thus presented as a part of the social construct: its principles must be mediated through that construct rather than being idealist truths which are latent within the individual and find a direct response there. There is a parallel to this rather surprisingly undogmatic treatment of religion in *Die Narrenburg*. Chelion, having followed Jodok from India, where she was an untouchable, is simply unable to exist in a foreign value system. It is important to note that Stifter is implying no condescension here: he can recognise the reality of a society governed by non-Christian principles as being alternative rather than simply heathen, which suggests that he accepts that even in Austria, these Christian principles operate as a part of the mechanics of the social construct rather than as an absolute, metaphysical set of references.

In the opening paragraph of *Turmalin* the narrator talks of 'dem inneren

---

[10] M. & E. Swales, op. cit., p. 181.

Gesetze, das ihn [den Menschen] unabwendbar zu dem Rechten führt' (p. 135). The story suggests that actually this 'innere Gesetz' is established only by participation in society, and that retreat from the social forces which thus constitute him must spell self-destruction.

*Turmalin* is exceptional in the context of *Bunte Steine* and indeed in Stifter's work as a whole, in that nature, and the accompanying concept of a 'sanftes Gesetz' is not a dominant aspect of the story. To some extent it is therefore free of one of the main objections which has always been raised about according Stifter Realist status, as, for example, by Zenker: 'Der mit leidenschaftlicher Naturliebe begabte Stifter ware gewiß ein großer Realist geworden, wenn nicht der Glaube an ein imaginäres "sanftes Gesetz" ihn der Wirklichkeit entfremdet hätte.'[11]

The idea that man fits into a universal system, that there is a metaphysical unity between mankind and the natural world, certainly seems initially to be a long way from conforming to an understanding of Realism which assigns it a rejection of the concept that man has any worth or identity beyond his socially defined and constructed ones. The security and stability which Stifter implies in such a system, characterized in the 'Vorrede' to *Bunte Steine* by his denial of the significance of occasional, dramatic events in the face of those less striking but enduring rhythms of nature, is immense. It does seem to be at odds with a conception of the world which offers the individual no security, not even the prospect of a human existence, outside of his social context.

This overwhelming affirmation of long-term stability is, as Swales and Swales have noted,[12] reflected even in the structure of a tale such as *Granit*, a 'Rahmenerzählung' based on a circular walk which culminates in the reconstruction of domestic peace after the initial turmoil between the boy and his mother. The inner story, too, although it deals with a terrible upheaval in the form of a plague, concludes on a note of reconstructed harmony. In both stories (see Swales and Swales, p. 145) time is seen to heal all wounds, a characterization of chronological progress which constitutes an absolutely fundamental affirmation of stability, and which is also reflected in the wisdom of the grandfather, a wisdom which is clearly the result of the process of ageing, of the experience of the passing of time. The stone before the house is symbolic of the unity of man and the natural world, and of the stability implied in that unity: it has been sat upon by members of the same family throughout living memory. Likewise, the repeated

---

[11] Zenker, op. cit., 109.

[12] M. & E. Swales, op. cit., pp. 142 - 55.

enumeration of aspects of the natural surroundings and of human influences in the landscape - the smoke in the woods, the villages, all pointed out by the grandfather and affirmed by the boy - emphasises the constancy of the human/natural unity from generation to generation.

The Grandfather's role is not undermined by Stifter's characterizing him, with a pinch of rare humour, as rather dogmatic and boring: that the boy already knows something does not deter him from teaching him it, as, for example, when on their way back home, he describes a lake:

> 'Das ist der See, Großvater, den ich im heraufgehen genannt habe', sagte ich, 'die Großmutter hat uns von seinem Wasser erzählt und den seltsamen Fischen die darin sind, und wenn ein weißes Wölklein über ihm steht, so kommt ein Gewitter.'
> 'Und wenn ein weißes Wölklein über ihn steht', fuhr der Großvater fort, 'und sonst heiterer Himmel ist, so gesellen sich immer mehrere dazu, es wird ein Wolkenheer, und das löst sich von dem Walde los und zieht zu uns mit dem Gewitter heraus, das uns den schweren Regen bringt und auch öfter den Hagel.' (p. 46).

It is a very gentle irony, similar to that injected into the woman's narration in *Turmalin*, and it can hardly be interpreted as pejorative: rather, it confirms the grandfather's humanity, and reinforces him as being a personification of order and certainty.

In *Granit*, then, Stifter does really seem to have constructed his longed for stability, to have accorded human existence the 'Sinn' which *Turmalin* appears to doubt it has. Is this, however, at the expense of his integrity as a Realist? Undeniable though it is that stories like *Granit* are clearly designed to provide mankind with a metaphysical framework which is as solid as the narrative framework in the tale itself, this does not in fact strip Stifter's work of its basic realist conception of human existence. This is because his stories suggest consistently that the overall unity he wants to believe in is subject to a crucial qualification, one which has been generally neglected in the critical literature. This is that man can only participate in it if he fulfils his role in human society. The individual thus cannot appeal directly to a metaphysical system: the legitimacy of his existence is measured only in terms of function, and this idea of function, just as in *Turmalin*, relates exclusively to the human system. The idea of 'Sinn' which life is accorded by man's place in the natural order of things operates only if man has found his place in the human order of things , and the individual who fails to do this is therefore denied a meaningful existence just as he is in mainstream

German Realism.

Stifter's work is littered with portraits of hermits, recluses, exiles who fail precisely because, however deeply they may bury themselves in nature, they, like the Rentherr, neglect their social identity: Abdias, the Hagestolz, a whole family line in *Die Narrenburg*, the Waldgänger and his first wife: all demonstrate powerfully that exclusion from the social order entails exclusion from the universal order; it is in effect fatal. It is certainly simplistic to suggest that Stifter simply advocates rural life as being 'healthier' than urban life: even in *Granit* he makes it clear that seclusion is no guarantee of security: 'Man hatte ... erzählt, wie in anderen Ländern eine Krankheit sei ...: aber niemand hatte geglaubt, daß sie in unsere Wälder hereinkommen werde, weil nie etwas Fremdes zu uns hereinkommt, bis sie kam' (p. 37). Those who flee the pest by seeking refuge away from the villages - in nature - do so in vain. Stifter, recognising that man's success in the human world is crucial, attempts to lend this success metaphysical significance by identifying it as the precursor to his finding his place in the natural world. This he illustrates in *Granit* by employing the pathetic fallacy: while he is telling the boy about the dark days of the plague the grandfather perceives it as being cold enough to warrant buttoning up the boy's jacket, whereas soon afterwards, on their arrival home, as the inner story nears its happy resolution, and the restoration of domestic harmony approaches, he suggests that 'da es so warm ist, so setzen wir uns ein wenig auf den Stein, ich werde dir die Geschichte zu Ende erzählen' (p. 57). Whether we understand that it has actually grown warmer, or simply that the Grandfather and the boy are imposing their perceptions onto nature, the message is the same. The theme of the disastrous consequences of isolation which is treated in *Turmalin* is by no means in opposition, then, to Stifter's ideal of a meaningful universe, for it, too, conforms to the premise that social integration is a condition of integration in the universal order, of meaningfulness.

However, we can go further than this if we separate the two aspects of Stifter's outlook which so clearly characterize his stories: on the one hand, the radical recognition of man as a purely socially contrived entity, and, on the other, his desire for reassurance in the shape of 'Sinn'. We return to a reading of his work in which the importance of social integration is not that without it the individual is rendered invalid because he is denied access to the greater, metaphysical system, rather that an individual outside of society simply has no real existence whatsoever, irrespective of more ethereal considerations: he has dissolved the clay out of which he has been moulded. The idea of a universal harmony is rendered irrelevant to this view of existence, for man is defined only by his immediately human context: whether we understand it as a serious philosophical construct, or as a mere sop to Stifter's need for deeper meaning and a guarantee of stability, it does not actually colour his presentation of his characters as quintessentially social animals.

*Katzensilber*, another story in which nature is a dominant feature, seems initially to resist such an interpretation. It is possible, indeed, to read it as an assertion of the supremacy of nature and an indictment of human society. Thus the family, corrupted by their winter visits to the city, are at odds with their rural environment, feverishly rebuilding each time the house is damaged by the elements. There is a lack of humanity apparent in the frequency with which the parents overlook the 'braunes Mädchen', despite her rescue of the children. If we see the 'braunes Mädchen' as the embodiment of humanity at one with nature, from which she always emerges and into which she finally retreats, and in which she is so at home, then her spontaneous kindness and her ability to protect the family's children may be seen to contrast with the selfishness of the family and their helplessness in the face of the force of nature as manifested in the storm and the fire. Their inability to accept nature on its own terms is indicated by their desire to integrate the 'braunes Mädchen' into their society, to reward her in material terms and give her a function: 'wir werden die Art schon finden, wie wir das Kind belohnen und ihm sein Leben vielleicht nützlicher machen können, als es jetzt ahnt' (p. 274). Ultimately she flees their society, just as the goblin does in the grandmother's fairytale, when he too is rewarded in material terms by the people whose goats he tends. This criticism of materialism also seems apparent in another of her fairytales, when a carbuncle, removed from the natural realm and sold into the human one, becomes the booty of conquering armies and an object of envy, and in the fact that the children can only express their affection for the 'braunes Mädchen' by giving her gifts: she, in contrast, 'hatte ihnen nichts zu geben und hielt die leeren Hände hin' (p. 282); her friendship for the children is nevertheless of much more value to them than their gifts ever are to her.

At the very least, then, *Katzensilber* reflects Stifter's mixed feelings about the character of social man. It does not follow, however, that he argues for a dissolution of this structure and a retreat into the 'purity' of nature. It is in this respect that Stifter is both Realist and realistic: *Katzensilber* ultimately affirms once again that, imperfect though the social system may be, it is the only context in which it is possible to pursue a human existence. The natural order is seen to be inaccessible to the asocial individual.

It is made clear in the story that the children are closer to nature, that they can better relate to the 'braunes Mädchen' than their parents can. In *Granit*, too, the boy's eyes are sharper than those of his grandfather. It may seem that for children, at least, the unmediated response to nature is still a possibility, although it is equally clear that the children are already firmly anchored to the family and its value system; hence the gift giving. The significant point is that as they grow up, their progress away from the world of the 'braunes Mädchen' and into the world of society is seen to be necessary and irreversible. One is reminded of Schiller's concept of the naive and the sentimental and the hopelessness of returning to the naive state, and of course, of the situation of Effi Briest, mentioned above. Mark Ward describes that scenario in the following terms: 'The "Naturkind" Effi ... has two routes out of the garden: one into a cemetery, the other into the social world of the house, a social world which is clearly inimicable to her childlike nature and, of course, it is clear that she cannot spend the rest of her life in the garden.' [13] The retreat of the 'braunes Mädchen' is as inevitable as Effi's exit from the garden, for she becomes irrelevant in the social world into which the children must now emerge. Now the parallel with the fairytale of the goblin becomes more illuminating. His goats, just like the children, are described in terms of their colour: 'sowohl weiße als schwarze, sowohl scheckige als braune' (p. 249), while the children are 'Schwarzköpfchen', 'Blondköpfchen' and 'Braunköpfchen'. As they grow older, the children's increasing beauty is stressed; likewise, the goats 'werden immer schöner' (p. 249). Both the goblin and the 'braunes Mädchen', then, disappear when their charges have 'ripened' and when attempts are made to draw them into the materialist social world themselves.

The parallel between the two is furthered by their fairy tale associations, an aspect of the story treated by Eve Mason. [14] The fact that the 'braunes Mädchen' is so connotative of both the natural and the fairy tale worlds adds to the evidence that she represents a stage which is necessarily transient, and indeed is literally unreal for the adult human being. Naming the children 'Schwarz-', 'Blond-' and 'Braunköpfchen' also invokes the fairy tale mode, and it is significant that in the end, when the children are seen to start participating in the social world, these

---

[13] Ward, op. cit., 85.

[14] E. Mason, 'Stifter's *Katzensilber* and the Fairy-Tale Mode'. *MLR*, 77 (1982), 114 - 29.

terms are dropped, while the grandmother - who, as she ages by implication becomes a socially less functional entity (she is, for example, no longer needed to look after the children) - is now described as 'ein Weißköpfchen ... unter den Kindern' (p. 312). The last words of the 'braunes Mädchen' before she runs off for ever also refer directly to the fairy tale, for 'Sture Mure ist tot' (p. 313) is an echo from the grandmother's first story about the 'braune Magd', who flees on hearing that the farmer has been told 'sag der Sture Mure, die Rauh-Rinde sei tot' (p. 248).

It is wrong, then, to compare the failure of the attempts to integrate the 'braunes Mädchen' with the relative success of the integration of the daughter in *Turmalin.* The latter figure is an example of a distorted human being, whereas the 'braunes Mädchen' is much more symbolic, standing for something which must be left behind if the children are to grow up into the social world. Requadt summarizes the *Bunte Steine* as follows: 'Menschen, meist aus ländlicher Umgebung, werden einer Natur- oder Geschichtskatastrophe ausgesetzt. Die Erwachsenen können sie bestehen oder vor ihnen versagen, in jedem Fall werden die Kinder gerettet, und ein neuer Zustand bahnt sich an.'[15] This pattern is rendered significant, and indeed radical, only when we recognize that the survival of the adults depends on their acceptance of a social function, while the survival of the children is accompanied by their growth out of their naive, pre-social state towards the socially integrated condition which is the definition of the adult human being.

Whether or not the 'braunes Mädchen' is in fact postulated as an actuality is doubtful; she is certainly irrelevant to Stifter's view of the adult world. The same is true of Stifter's concept of universal harmony: the decisive context is always the social one. Ultimately, the 'braunes Mädchen' is just a fond memory, a yearning, in Sigismund. Stifter's insistence on the necessity of social integration is so rigorous that it seems fair to conclude that his 'sanftes Gesetz', his constant invoking of the authority of nature and its attendant order, represents no more than such a yearning in him, a 'memory' of a more stable world which his stories actually show to be redundant.

---

[15] P. Requadt, 'Stifters *Bunte Steine* als Zeugnis der Revolution und als zyklisches Kunstwerk' in *Adalbert Stifter: Studien und Interpretationen,* ed. L. Stiehm, (Heidelberg, 1968), p. 55.

# 'Ein schwer definierbares Ragout': Ida Hahn-Hahn's *Gräfin Faustine* -

# Vapours from the *Hexenküche* or Social and Psychological Realism?

by Helen Chambers

The canon of German realist writing despite increasing research into nineteenth-century women's writing remains not only male-dominated, but an almost exclusively male preserve. Droste-Hülshoff and Ebner-Eschenbach are so far the only women from the period whose works figure in the publisher Reclam's list which is a relatively progressive barometer of the current state of German literary studies. In order to modify the received wisdom it is important to identify works of appropriate literary value whose neglect has been contingent on historical factors which are due to be swept aside. Against this background, I would argue the case for the acceptance of Ida Hahn-Hahn's novel *Gräfin Faustine* (1841) as a significant contribution to the German realist novel, taking as my frame of reference Martin Swales' definition of realism as '[entailing] ... not mere accuracy and fidelity to detail but truth, and part of the truth must ... derive from the ways in which human beings feel, think, and understand themselves and their experience - and from the fact that, in their feeling and thinking, even as private individuals, they are implicated in the value structure of their society'. [1] I shall equally argue the case for the modernity of text and explore further the feasibility of a feminist reading, as it is a work that has caused problems for feminists and male traditionalists alike.

In her afterword to the 1986 Bouvier edition Annemarie Taeger highlights the widespread critical misreading of the novel, and it is thus not without misgivings that I first proffer a synopsis of the text. [2] *Gräfin Faustine* opens on the Brühlsche Terrasse in Dresden. Young men sit smoking and gossipping in the sun while a few yards away a young woman of quality sits on a bench with her back to them drawing, absorbed in her work. She is Gräfin Faustine Obernau, a widow whose constant companion Baron Anastas Andlau awaits her in her apartments. A letter arrives inviting her to her brother-in-law's country estate to become godmother to the youngest of her sister's numerous children. The prospect of separation from Andlau, to whom she is not married for reasons to be revealed later, depresses her, and it is with relief that she returns to Dresden again after a large dose of domesticity at Oberwalldorf with her family. Some months later Andlau is forced by family duties to leave her for a prolonged period during which she gradually and largely unwittingly allows Graf Mario Mengen, an intelligent and attractive diplomat, to replace Andlau in her affections. Mengen in turn has to leave Dresden, for a family wedding, and on the eve of his departure he pressurises her into declaring her love for him and into writing a letter of farewell to Andlau. In the course of the evening Faustine tells Mengen the story of her past: she has first met her friend and lover Andlau in her marital home. She has been married off at the age of seventeen to a wealthy, handsome, but as it turns out, brutal husband, ten years her senior. Andlau gives her a sense of her own worth, encouraging her to develop as an individual. One day however her husband shoots and wounds Andlau having surprised them together in what appears to be a compromising situation. This is Faustine's cue to leave Obernau and after nursing Andlau back to health she travels to Italy with him where she experiences a new life, 'Im Doppellicht des Lebens und der Kunst' and as she puts it, '... wie entwickelten sich meine Fähigkeiten! ... wie sicher, wie bewußt meines Glücks und meines Rechts daran stand ich im Nachen und ließ ihn durch Andlau lenken!' (p. 195) She explains that despite her husband's death, she has not become Andlau's wife

---

[1] M. W. Swales. '"Neglecting the Weight of the Elephant ...": German Prose Fiction and European Realism', *MLR*, 83 (1988), 894.

[2] Ida Hahn-Hahn, *Gräfin Faustine*, (Bonn, 1986).

as her two years of marriage have been too traumatic for her to contemplate another attempt. Andlau respects her wishes and recognises her need to develop in freedom. Mengen however, blinded or perhaps deafened by love, only focuses on the fact that she has no formal commitment to another, and since she has admitted she loves him and Andlau is elsewhere, the case seems clear-cut to him. He begs her to be his wife and despite her manifest anxiety at the thought he steamrollers her, less by the archetypally male set of arguments he advances than by sheer force of personality. She does insist on not leaving with him immediately to meet his parents however, as she wants assurance first that they will welcome her. We have a brief view of Andlau receiving his farewell letter in Nürnberg and riding off in distraction to Prague, Breslau and Cracov, from where he replies to her with altruistic resignation. During Mengen's absence Faustine reflects honestly on what she has done, concluding, 'Es gibt keinen Stillstand für mich, rastlos muß ich vorwärts - und ist das nicht eins und dasselbe mit aufwärts? -' (p. 207) and returning to her social and artistic pursuits. She is visited by her younger brother-in-law Clemens who has fallen in love with her and who misconstrues her sympathy as potential affection. She views the advances of this large powerful man with alarm, but without losing her composure. He presses her to reveal whom she loves, and when she indicates it is Mengen he is devastated and returning the following day ostensibly to take his leave he grasps her wrist in his left hand and shoots himself. She faints and it is thus that Mengen finds her and instantly bears her off to his family home.

The first two hundred or so pages, more than nine tenths of the novel, have been recounted by a relatively sympathetic but discreet narrative voice, mediating reality to the reader predominantly but not exclusively from Faustine's point of view and only occasionally obtruding as an unidentified contemporary 'ich' who interpolates a number of discursive reflections prompted by the developments narrated. After the account of Clemens' suicide and the apparent closure of Mengen and Faustine's decision to marry, there is a seven-year break in the narrative and a complete shift of perspective. The new narrator who takes over is a figure in the novel, a countess who meets Mengen by chance at the graveside of Leopold Robert[3] in Venice. She has an unidentified taciturn male companion, and during eight days in Venice the pensive Mengen, who has his and Faustine's lively six-year-old son Bonaventura with him, unfolds to this woman the story of his marriage and of Faustine's death. Despite their reciprocal love and her own

---

[3] Swiss romantic painter (1794 - 1835) who committed suicide.

outstanding professional success as an artist, she has been unable to sustain her positive, dynamic attitude to life. Mengen's attempts to turn her into a socially acceptable good wife and mother have failed. A journey to the Orient, which he at first tries to deny her, has only had the effect of convincing her that she has no more to experience in this world and she becomes subject to increasing melancholy. In Pisa she is re-united with Andlau on his death-bed - he dies as a consequence of the old wound from her first husband. She feels mentally and spiritually drained, excluded from the higher spheres of enthusiasm and imagination and thus decides that further development of her inner self can only be pursued through religion in devotion to God. She has her marriage annulled and enters a convent in Rome. Mengen does not see her again, but when she dies a year and a half later he is convinced that she has not found the peace in God she sought, but has died of despair at the constraint she has imposed on her 'unbändige Natur' (p. 239).

When Mengen has told this tale in the form of an extended flashback without interruption he takes his leave and the final paragraph of the novel is spoken by the new narrator to her silent companion. It takes the form of a generalised reflection on women like Faustine, and is a highly critical reading of the life we have been shown, and one which identifies with the male figures as victims of what the opinionated narrator condemns as the vampire nature of Faustine - 'solche feingeistige Vampirnatur verbrennt und verbraucht - zuerst den andern, dann sich selbst' (p. 244) and exhorts a clearly male audience to beware of such creatures as there is no cure for their insatiableness, and their promise of undying emotional commitment is an illusion. Thus the final block of narrative, by being told in the first person by Mengen and being framed by comments from a figure who sympathises with his fate and views Faustine as a dangerous aberration runs counter to the thrust of the rest of the work, in which a more neutral or sympathetic view of the protagonist is mediated. It is a radical shift which disorientates the reader and should give him/her pause for thought. However all too often the second narrator's commentary has been taken at face value by critics as the key to the rest of the work. Indeed the last word in the novel, 'Dämon', has given rise to an inordinate amount of criticism involving a reading of Faustine's character as demonic. [4]

The deliberate ambiguity created by the broken narrative perspective is such

---

[4] See, for example, Fr. Sengle, *Biedermeierzeit. Deutsche Literatur im Spannungsfeld zwischen Restauration und Revolution 1815 - 1848*, (Stuttgart, 1971), Bd. I, 279; H. Mayer, *Außenseiter*, (Frankfurt am Main, 1977), pp. 76 - 82.

that it demands the interpretative involvement of the reader, whom it calls on to decode the narrative and come to a conclusion beyond that proposed by the ostensibly authoritative narrative voice at the end. It is an earlier example of what Mark Ward refers to in the case of Storm's *Der Schimmelreiter* as 'the interpretative and evaluative uncertainty surround[ing] Hauke Haien - progressive visionary or diabolical tyrant?' [5] It is not unrelated technically to the endings of other German realist narratives, such as Keller's *Romeo und Julia auf dem Dorfe* where the last words, cited from a self-righteously condemnatory newspaper item on the protagonists' suicide are radically at odds with the interpretation of events suggested by the narrative perspective in the main body of the story. Similarly the ending of Droste-Hülshoff's *Judenbuche* produces a pat formula for judging what has gone before which is far from consonant with the thrust and complexity of the narrative. All these cases point to a characteristic reflex of German realist writing whereby a judgement or the advancement of a solution at the end of a narrative underscores the problematic nature of values in view of the complex social and psychological texture of the real world as mediated by the work.

One of the problems involved in evaluating Faustine as a figure and a novel is that it appears to have activated a recoil reflex in a number of readers, which has given rise to some very extreme or partial readings. There is not scope within the present framework to analyse the reception history of the novel in detail but one or two samples may be instructive. [6] A number of male readers see the character as arrogant and self-obsessed, others see her as mad, and/or emotionally and sexually insatiable. Friedrich Sengle is particularly prone to biased, subjective readings. In Faustine's case he is a master of the inappropriate epithet. Under the rubric 'Weltschmerz' he comments: 'Man glaubt der christlichen Droste, die manches mit den Weltschmerzpoeten verbindet, ihren Zweifel im *Geistlichen Jahr* eher als der tollen Gräfin ihre faustische Verzweiflung.' [7] The fact that Sengle, subjectively, finds it easier to identify with Droste does not of course mean that the countess is mad, she is not, nor is her despair faustian strictly speaking. The heroine owes her name to her father's obsession with the great male work of the great German male and one should surely pause before equating this character too glibly with a paternally imposed role model. Taeger puts her finger more

---

[5] M. G. Ward, '"Only an Elephant can bear an Elephant's Burden": German Realism - The Limits and Limitations of Liberal Reading', *NGS*, 16 (1990/91), 89.

[6] Cf Katrien von Munster, *Die junge Gräfin Hahn-Hahn*, Diss., (Nimwegen, 1929), and Annemarie Taeger's afterword to the Bouvier edition, op. cit., pp. 249ff.

[7] Sengle, op. cit., Bd. I, 235.

appositely on the nature of Faustine's restlessness and longing when she writes:
'Von Faustine heißt es, das Streben selbst sei "ihr alleinziges Glück"; nicht der am
Ergebnis orientierte, sondern der an der Kraft des Verlangens gemessene
Lebensentwurf verspricht Befriedigung. Seligkeit liegt in der Fähigkeit zum
Wunsch als Antrieb zur Tat.'[8] Sengle however fails to differentiate except in crass
terms and produces the following account of the novel and its protagonist: 'Diese
weibliche Abart Fausts ... ist Universalpoetin, Malerin, Dichterin, vor allem aber
Universalerotikerin. Sie wechselt die Männer, wobei grelle Effekte nicht gescheut
werden. Der junge Clemens Walldorf erschießt sich vor ihren Augen, als er sieht,
daß sie Graf Mengen bevorzugt. Die Liebe, meint sie, kommt der Kunst zugute.
Trotz solcher romantischer Einsprengsel ist die Geschichte von dieser wilden
Gräfin eigentlich ein weiblicher Schelmenroman ... Wie es sich bei dieser Gattung
gehört, endet die Heldin im Kloster.'[9] Patricia Herminghouse observes with
restraint: 'Like many before him, Sengle prefers to indulge in a display of
misogynistic humour rather than engage in a serious examination of Hahn-Hahn
as a writer.'[10] He has probably taken his cue from Eichendorff who likewise
oversimplifies the plot to her going through a series of men and leaving the last
one and her child to become a nun. Eichendorff does this however in an essay
published in a periodical, not in a major literary historical work.[11] In addition
Eichendorff's cards are clearly on the table. He writes out of a sense of moral
outrage at her perceived self-indulgence, and as a Catholic who cannot accept her
unorthodox attitude to religion: 'Sie hat genossen das irdische Glück, ist blasiert,
und sucht nun höchst gelangweilt, statt des weltlichen Genusses einen pikanteren,
gleichwie ein Weinsäufer zuletzt zum Schnapse greift.'
    These strikingly distorted negative responses should of course be seen in the
context of Hahn-Hahn's huge success as a best-selling writer in her own time,[12]

---

[8] Taeger, op. cit., p. 253.

[9] Sengle, op. cit., Bd. II, 882.

[10] P. A. Herminghouse, 'Seeing Double: Ida Hahn-Hahn (1805 - 1880) and
her Challenge to Feminist Criticism' in *Out of Line/Ausgefallen: The Paradox of
Marginality in the Writings of Nineteenth-Century German Women*, ed. R.-E.
Boetcher Joeres and M. Burkhard, (Amsterdam, 1989), p. 258.

[11] Joseph von Eichendorff, 'Die deutsche Salon-Poesie der Frauen' in
*Sämtliche Werke*, ed. H. Schulhof et al, (Regensburg, 1923ff.), Bd. VIII/I, 70 - 80,
first published in *Historisch-politische Blätter für das katholische Deutschland*, 19
(1847), 463 - 80.

[12] See E. Sagarra, 'Gegen den Zeit- und Revolutionsgeist. Ida Gräfin Hahn-
Hahn und die christliche Tendenzliteratur im Deutschland des 19. Jahrhunderts' in
*Deutsche Literatur von Frauen*, ed. G. Brinker-Gabler, (Munich, 1988), II, 105 - 19.

and there can be little doubt that she appealed to women readers particularly - though one would be interested to discover the evidence for Sengle's claim that her books were preferred reading in girls' boarding schools, whereas adults read 'her model' George Sand instead. [13] On the occasion of Ida Hahn-Hahn's visit to England in 1846 Robert Browning wrote to Elizabeth Barrett of the novel: 'What a horrible book ... such characters as Faustine produce the worst possible effect on me ... contempt would be the most christian of all the feelings possible to be called forth by such a woman!' Elizabeth however replied: 'But there is much beauty in Faustina - Oh, surely!', [14] and in 1858 she wrote in a letter about her attempts to learn German: 'Heaps of Mme Hahn Hahn's novels have been consumed in this endeavour.' [15] They appealed to Jane Welsh Carlyle too, for she wrote in a letter in 1843: '... read in the dreamy novels of the Gräfin Hahn Hahn (Countess Cock Cock! What a name!) She is a sort of German George Sand *without the genius* - and *en revanche* a good deal more of what we call in Scotland *gumtion* - a clever woman really - separated from her husband of course - and on the whole very good to read when one is in a state of moral and physical collapse.' [16]

Despite this evidence it would be wrong to assume that Ida Hahn-Hahn's works inevitably appeal to women and repel men. The *Edinburgh Review* of January 1844 carries an article by the barrister, essayist and Faust translator Abraham Hayward which gives an account of six of her novels and begins by asserting her pre-eminent quality and originality in a Germany which he describes as 'Rich in historians, fertile in critics, abounding in metaphysicians, and overflowing with thinkers, (or gentlemen who think they are thinking) but which for the past quarter of a century has been utterly unable to produce a writer of prose fiction who does not turn out to be an imitator'. He dismisses the customary comparisons with Geroge Sand and gives a fair account of *Gräfin Faustine* based on judicious quotation, commenting however on the character of Faustine: 'This, it must be allowed, is a fine but wild conception; and it may be true that there is

---

[13] Sengle, op. cit., I, 235.

[14] *The Letters of Robert Browning and Elizabeth Barrett Barrett 1845 - 1846*, ed. E. Kintner, (Cambridge, Mass., 1969), II, 805ff.

[15] *Elizabeth Barrett Browning's Letters to Mrs. David Ogilvy 1849 - 1861*, ed. P. N. Heydon and P. Kelly, (New York, 1973), p. 148.

[16] Jane Carlyle to Jeannie Welsh, 2 October 1843, in *The Collected Letters of Thomas and Jane Carlyle*, ed. C. de Ryals and K. J. Fielding, (Durham and London, 1990), XVII.

nothing in actual life resembling it; - even in Germany, where all varieties of female character are to be found in much greater plenty than in any other country.'[17]

This raises the question of the subject matter of realism in general and in respect of this novel in particular. The *Athenaeum* reviewer of *The Countess Faustina* (trs. by N.S. London, 1844) adopts an unambiguous stance : 'As a picture of life too the story fails; the heroine being a prodigy.'[18] Can a realist narrative have as its protagonist a character who is portrayed as a highly gifted non-conformer, and additionally be set in an aristocratic milieu? If one looks at later texts in the realist canon the answer would appear to be yes. Storm's Hauke Haien for example is set apart from his contemporaries by his intellect, aspirations and unconventionality, and as to social setting - Renate Möhrmann's description of Hahn-Hahn's fictional world as 'die Welt der Salons und der Parks, der Reunionen und Soireen, der Medisancen und Fadaisen'[19] reads like an account of many characteristic scenes in Fontane. In *Gräfin Faustine* both these potentially exclusive, élitist elements are combined, but closer scrutiny reveals that these are concomitant rather than fundamental aspects of the social and psychological reality Hahn-Hahn presents. Although she writes about her own social milieu, which happens to be upper class, and she is the first German novelist to do so from first hand experience, in *Gräfin Faustine* her characters are shown interacting in the private and domestic sphere in the main, and not at glittering or exclusive formal and public occasions. It is therefore unhelpful to use the term *Salonroman* for example, which tends to isolate the work in a narrowly specific genre, when in fact it fits easily into the broad sweep of the novel of social and psychological realism.

What interests Hahn-Hahn is human behaviour and interaction,[20] and this is what she shows us, particularly in terms of the interrelationships between the sexes, of gender-specific differences of approach, and of the power politics of sexual difference. This kind of interaction of the sexes is not exclusive to one particular class. Women's reality in the nineteenth century inevitably involved

---

[17] A. Hayward, 'The Countess of Hahn-Hahn's Writings', *Edinburgh Review*, 79 (January 1844), 173.

[18] *Athenaeum*, 22 March 1845, 289.

[19] *Frauenemanzipation im deutschen Vormärz*, ed. R. Möhrmann, (Stuttgart, 1978), p. 231.

[20] Cf. Ida Hahn-Hahn, *Von Babylon nach Jerusalem*, (Mainz, 1851), p. 25: 'Ich wollte verstehen und erkennen - ja, was denn so eigentlich? Den Menschen!'

power relationships with men, where patterns of dominance and subservience were worked out in the main verbally, that is in the medium of conversation. The greater part of *Gräfin Faustine* is taken up by conversations, mostly between male and female interlocutors. On the matter of the class milieu Annemarie Taeger observes: 'Gräfin Faustine ist, trotz des Adelstitels in einer bürgerlichen Atmosphäre angesiedelt, die einen realistischen Erzählduktus eher als einen phantastischen zuläßt' (p. 260), and it is certainly the case that the milieus depicted in the two excursions from Dresden that we witness, her visit to her sister's and to Graf Feldern's fiancée Kunigunde are designed to show conventional family configurations and values which are as typical of the middle as of the upper class. The assumptions regarding marriage, motherhood and women's acquiescence within the hierarchical structure span the boundaries of class. Graf Mengen's aspirations for his gifted wife sound dishearteningly bourgeois: 'Meinen Erziehungsprojekten zufolge sollte sie sich aber an den geregelten einförmigen Gang der Existenz im Verkehr mit anderen wie in der bürgerlichen Stellung gewöhnen' (p. 228).

Ida Hahn-Hahn rejected the conventional representation of an idealised heroine, behaving as a model of female virtue, or regretting it bitterly if she did not. However if the heroine portrayed here is exceptional in terms of her artistic gifts (she stops short of classing herself a genius) her problems are not extraordinary at all, but ordinary human problems of the relationships of the self to the other, be that other accepted codes of behaviour, men or art and religion. If, to quote J. M. Ritchie, 'Fontane is too much of a realist ever to see only one side of any question; hence ambiguities, ambivalences, polarities, are the hallmark of all his writing',[21] then this is already equally true of Hahn-Hahn writing *Gräfin Faustine*. Without wishing to labour the comparison, in Faustine Hahn-Hahn has already created a heroine who is, like Effi Briest, pre-eminently 'liebenswürdig', who knows that she lacks 'Grundsätze' (p. 17), and who ends up marrying a man who having been attracted by her very freshness and spontaneity, sets about trying to teach her to be something less natural, individualistic and self-assured.

There can be no doubt that in terms of its subject matter, this novel fulfils Martin Swales' criterion for realism. It is less about outer action and empirically observable objects than about 'the ways in which human beings feel, think and understand themselves and their experience', and it is consonant with his view of the role of milieu, namely that the characters 'in their feeling and thinking even as

---

[21] *The Age of Realism*, ed. F. W. Hemmings, (Hassocks, 1978), p. 253.

private individuals are implicated in the value structure of their society'.[22]

So much for the subject matter, but what of the literary qualities, the aesthetic form? These have already been touched on in terms of the ambiguity of the text, which is one of its strengths, and as with many later realist writers, humour and irony are important aspects of Hahn-Hahn's technique for mediating the incongruities of the far from ideal reality she portrays. There is not scope here for a detailed stylistic analysis of the text, but commentary on a few characteristic extracts may serve to highlight some of its more interesting features. Critics, as Herminghouse too has pointed out, have gone through contorsions in the attempt to locate Hahn-Hahn in the appropriate literary historical category, in the company of fitting literary bedfellows. Sengle, for example says she is a stew-up of Byron, Jean Paul and French influences.[23] Romanticism, classicism, Biedermeier, Young Germany and realism are invoked. As a work from the first half of the nineteenth century which does yield evidence of a variety of literary currents, but not at the cost of its own coherence, it is a rewarding text for study and for cutting analytical teeth on.

It cannot be denied that there are passages in the novel which are characterised by pathos and cliché to an extent that may cause problems for the modern reader. However it is important to see these in conjunction with the other more sober, apparently more controlled passages with which they are juxtaposed; to consider their role in the overall development of the narrative, and not to overlook the ironic dimension inherent in the integration of these passages into the novel as a whole. On the occasion of Andlau's, as it turns out fateful, departure we are all but spared the emotional exchange: 'Beim Abschied sprach er zu Faustinen, nachdem er alle Ausdrücke der Liebe und Zärtlichkeit erschöpft hatte: ...' Only the essential, forward-pointing exchange about her inability to forget him is included (pp. 78ff.). This is followed by an accomplished realistic evocation of a scene in Frau von Eilau's salon in terms of the disposition of the furniture and its relationship to social intercourse, and then of the ebb and flow of conversation without authorial comment, which by its subject matter discreetly explores and anticipates the developing themes of male/female relationships in the novel. Faustine's belated arrival then provides a dramatic focus, and the first stages of Mengen's love for her are humorously but tellingly conveyed as he tries to

---

[22] Swales, op. cit., 894.

[23] Sengle, op. cit., II, 881: 'In Wirklichkeit gibt sie [Hahn-Hahn] ein schwer definierbares Ragout aus Byron, Jean Paul und den französischen Einflüssen.'

glimpse her across a crowded room, constrained to immobility as he is by his beautiful chess partner, Lady Geraldin. Mengen is subjected to mockery by the narrative perspective in this scene, in a way that exposes him as a character who is not as much in control of women as he might think he is, whereas Faustine is shown to be in command of herself and the situation. Character, milieu and relationships are thus being explored and the foundations of future action laid, in what might at first sight appear to be no more than a descriptive set piece depicting the aristocratic salon of the period.

Hahn-Hahn's conversational technique is taken one stage further when Mengen's friend Graf Feldern's reluctant fiancée, Kunigunde, comes to visit Faustine for advice (pp. 118-22). This pivotal scene shows Faustine in action, that is in conversation, for apart from her painting, it is a function of her woman's role that speech is the only form of action open to her. She first of all makes the otherwise silent Kunigunde, who has been reduced to a state of virtual paralysis by her engagement to a man she does not love, articulate her feelings. They are sentiments which are not consonant with her role as dutiful daughter, beautiful but impoverished, with younger sisters to be married off after her. Faustine is seen first - to use modern parlance - counselling and supporting Kunigunde, adjusting the vocabulary she uses of her own behaviour from negative to positive: 'Nennen Sie Ihre Seele nicht schwach, sondern klar', and in the following conversation with the worthy but unloved Feldern Faustine counsels him, presenting him with a corrected view of Kunigunde and adjusting the terminology he unreflectingly applies to the situation. She replaces 'erlauben' with 'vergeben' in his formulation, thus shifting the male role from one of dominant mentor to one of sympathetic accepter of difference.

The sub-plot involving the attempted rescue of Kunigunde not only serves to show Faustine in action and to discuss central themes of the novel, it also has an important structural role to play. Faustine tries to release Kunigunde from the patriarchal structures of society and give her freedom to be herself, not simply a socially determined appendage of a socially acceptable male. The rescue however is effected by Mengen's assistance. She is found a position as companion to his sister, and this in the fulness of time, as Faustine bitterly recognises in the final section of the novel, turns out to be a worse trap than what she escaped from. The news comes that Kunigunde is to marry a clergyman of fashionably fanatical cast, a much worse option than the pleasant, considerate if conventional Feldern. Her motives are assumed to be *Torschlußpanik*. This thread thus runs parallel to the main plot in which Graf Mengen, who apparently represents a channel for the enabling of Faustine's further development, in fact proves to be her destruction, not her salvation, and a far worse option than Andlau whom she rejects. This particular model, represented here in dual form to suggest that Faustine's fate is not to be viewed as purely individual and atypical, epitomises a fundamental aspect of much realist writing, namely that by and large the human agents of misfortune and tragedy are not villains or men and women of evil design, but the well-intentioned. These bringers of disaster act frequently according to intentions of whose sources they themselves are unaware, but into whose mechanisms the narrative perspective affords critical insight. Mengen, for all his attractive and admirable qualities is bound by the prejudices of his sex and class. At the end he has seemingly no inkling of what he has done to Faustine. The later parallel figure of Innstetten in *Effi Briest* does acquire a degree of critical self-awareness in the course of the novel, but only after the damage has been done.

The scene in which Mengen brings Faustine the good news that he has found an escape route for Kunigunde is cliché-ridden: 'Er kniete neben ihr nieder und blickte glücklich in ihr Auge, aus welchem wieder der himmlische Strahl aufleuchtete. "O Mengen!" sagte sie nur, und legte die Hand auf die Brust; die andere gab sie ihm, und er behielt sie in den seinen, ohne sie zu küssen, lange friedlich, andächtig, immer wie verzaubert in ihr Antlitz schauend. Später drückte er heftig seine Lippen in die schmale zarte Hand' (p. 160). Read with hindsight as to the unfortunate outcome of this chivalrous service, however, the passage must appear in an ironic light, and it is already radically relativised by a paragraph which follows almost immediately after, in which the sober prose of reality is employed to describe what the rejected Feldern finds when he goes to the lodgings of Clemens, a parallel case of unrequited love. The sentimentally formulated, dewy-eyed hope for the future is thus immediately countered by an image of hopelessness and chaos in the present, couched in concrete, realistic terms:

> Feldern war geradewegs zu Clemens gegangen. Der breite Johann schien zweifelhaft, ob er ihn bei seinem Herrn einlassen solle oder nicht; da er aber bereits gesagt, er sei daheim, so mußte er ihm die Tür öffnen. Der zierliche, ordnungsliebende Feldern erschrak vor der Verwüstung, die in diesem großen, vielleicht ursprünglich eleganten Zimmer herrschte. Kleidungsstücke an der Erde, Teller auf den Stühlen, Flaschen, Karten, Überbleibsel vom Frühstück und von Zigarren auf den Tischen, Schläger und Pistolen auf dem Bett, Gläser überall, zwei Feldbettstellen nebeneinander aufgeschlagen, und

Clemens im Schlafrock, mit verwildertem Bart, geisterbleich, krankhaft, mitten im Zimmer stehend, den einen Arm um den Kopf geschlungen, der andere schlaff herabhängend. (p. 160)

One final extract may serve to confront the problem of the ambiguous and inconsistent nature of the text, of which Christine Lehmann has said: 'Der Text scheint zu schwanken zwischen dem Abklatsch romantischer Schwärmerei und radikalem Feminismus, und ist aus beiden Richtungen angreifbar.'[24] Mengen has just manipulated Faustine by a series of male strategies into saying she loves him, and as this admission causes her manifest anguish he has asked for an account of her past so that he can decide the matter (for her presumably):

'... Darum die Wahrheit, Herz, die reine Wahrheit, wie vor Gott.'
'Wie vor Gott!' wiederholte sie feierlich und stand auf. Sie waren schön, die beiden Gestalten einander gegenüber. Mario saß in seiner gewöhnlichen Stellung mit untergeschlagenen Armen seitwärts am Tisch, und die Kerzen warfen nut ein Streiflicht über ihn. Aber sein marmorbleicher Kopf mit den vornehm stolzen, aber durch die Macht der Empfindung für den Augenblick melancholischen Zügen, mit dem tiefen, geistreichen, glühenden Auge und dem dunklen Gelock, hob sich, gleich einem Gemälde von Velasquez oder Murillo, lebhaft von der dunkelroten Lehne des Fauteuils ab, welche ihn hoch überragte. Faustine stand vor ihm, im vollen Kerzenlicht, blaßrot gekleidet, blühend, weich, schwebend, halb sinnlich, halb seelisch, hingehaucht wie von Guido Renis Pinsel, etwas vom Johannes, etwas von der Magdalena im Ausdruck, der in jeder Sekunde wechselte, so wie sie die Skala der Gefühle durchflog. - Er - ruhig, fest, entschlossen, nicht unerschütterlich, aber kampfbereit und unermüdlich, die Siegesfahne tragend, vielleicht in den Tod, doch gewiß nicht in den Untergang. Sie - schwankend, und immer ungewiß lassend, ob sie fallen, ob sie in den Himmel auffliegen werde. Er - ganz Mann. Sie - ganz Weib. (p. 181)

Annemarie Taeger cites the above description of Faustine as an example of cliché and kitsch, which she argues are particularly evident when Hahn-Hahn abandons a critical 'Frauenperspektive' in favour of a more conciliatory portrayal (p. 261). However this reading can be challenged, for the purpleness of the passage must be seen in the light of Mengen's preceding direct assertion of his proprietary intentions: 'Ich will Sie haben, Faustine', and her equally direct recognition of the predicament she has got herself into: 'Das begreif' ich'

---

[24] C. Lehmann, *Das Modell Clarissa. Liebe, Verführung, Sexualität und Tod der Romanheldinnen des 18. und 19. Jahrhunderts*, (Stuttgart, 1991), pp. 74 - 83, devotes a chapter to *Gräfin Faustine* which includes illuminating analysis of the conflicting discourses and stylistic inconsistencies in the text.

(p. 180). Thus the configuration of characters has been first presented in their own words in unadorned prosaic terms. It is against this that the poetic elaboration with its chiaroscura and rhetorical effects must be seen. Although it may cause initial queasiness in the contemporary reader, I would argue that the shift from prosaic to poetic intensity can be read as critical. Mengen's verbal transformation of her into an angel and himself by implication into God appears questionable from the reader's point of view. That the narrator portrays them as beautiful at this moment of suffusion by mutual passion does not exclude the simultaneous implied questioning of the viability of their relationship and the male/female balance within it. The comparison of Mengen to a Velasquez or Murillo - presumably to one of the formal male portraits - and of Faustine to the more sensual, ethereal creations of Guido Reni suggests the contrast between them. The fact that they do not belong in the same painting points forward to the dissolution of their marriage, even at the moment when they are seemingly about to be bound together by love. 'Er - ganz Mann. Sie - ganz Frau' is in this context a highly ambiguous formulation. It could be seen as a clichéd assertion of the perfect complementary balance of the sexes, but in the light of the social and psychological reality already established by the text it can more appropriately be read as the devastating assertion of the polarity of the terms, of the radical binary divide between the male and female perspective which is at the heart of the novel. This second reading is borne out by the ensuing exchange between the 'Mann' and the 'Weib'.

'"Rede, mein Engel," sagte Mario sanft; "Keine Frage, keine Einwendung, kein Blick soll dich stören."' This apparently gentle self-denying utterance in fact means that he has put her on a conventional pedestal, quite inappropriate to the story she tells, and that not only will he not enter into any dialogue about what he hears, he will not even listen to, or hear, its full import. He will blot out what he does not want to know. We then read Faustine's words: '"Was habe ich denn eigentlich zu sagen?" fragte Faustine sich selbst, träumerisch die Hand an die Stirn legend. "Alltägliche Schicksale, ein Leben ohne gewaltige Ereignisse, eine Persönlichkeit ohne überewiegende Vorzüge - das ward mir, das bin ich"', which on the one hand equally shows her not speaking directly to him, crossing the binary divide, and on the other articulates a typically female fate - not in the world of public life and action: 'das ward mir ...' and a typically female consciousness: namely self-evaluation in the form of self-deprecation, undervaluing of the self: '- das bin ich'. Thus what might at first sight appear to be a purple passage of kitsch and cliché has a critical impact to make in the economy of the narrative when read against its context. It does not nullify or contradict the more overt critical perspective of other parts of the narrative, it rather reinforces it by making strikingly visible the trap in which the female is all to readily caught by the language and attitudes of patriarchal society, which Hahn-Hahn convincingly recreates.

This brings us finally to consider briefly the problems *Gräfin Faustine* causes for feminist readers. Herminghouse poses but does not resolve this problem, disqualifying Hahn-Hahn by observing: 'We like our stories to have happy ends - preferably with positive heroines we can identify at least as proto-feminists.'[25] Hahn-Hahn is more often classed as pseudo-emancipatory than as the real thing, though Eichendorff's editor is more generous in designating her 'eine Vorkämpferin der Frauenemanzipation',[26] surely an apt description for the authoress of *Gräfin Faustine* which both implicitly and explicitly addresses and analyses the anti-woman mechanisms of society. For example Faustine pleads for dignity and self-esteem for women when she analyses a pervasive model of marriage: 'Den Ungeliebten zu beherrschen, ist eine Entwürdigung, weil nur zwei niedrige Mittel diese Herrschaft geben können: die Heuchelei der Frau, die Sinnlichkeit des Mannes ...' (p. 131) and sees its perniciousness not in loss of face before the world, but in loss of self-respect; or again when the narrator reflects on gender-specific attitudes, concluding that pity is something a woman feels for a man and not vice versa: '... die Frau hat viel mehr Wohlwollen für den Mann, in welchem sie von Hause aus eine Stütze und den Begründer ihres Glückes sieht, als er für sie hat, die er doch nur, à tout prendre, als eine Beute betrachtet' (p. 173).

Apart from the overt criticism and exposure of male attitudes in terms of the power and dominance of what are shown to be by and large the more ignorant, narrow-minded, insensitive and egotistical and generally less admirable sex over the more imaginative, humane and less hide-bound and self-centred female sex, the novel, despite its apparent woman-denying closure with Faustine's death, nonetheless goes beyond the not insignificant exposure of woman's position, to adumbrate the possibility of men's adopting conventionally female characteristics and roles. As Christine Lehmann points out, the opening of the novel shows Andlau waiting at home with a headache for his partner who has been out

---

[25] Herminghouse, op. cit., p. 276.

[26] See Note 11, p. 204.

working, and it is she who decides where they go and what they do. He is altogether far from being a stereotypical male character, although admittedly he dies as a direct result of stereotypical gender-specific behaviour by both Faustine and her husband. At the end of the novel, too, Mengen, having lost his wife as a result of his own insistence on asserting conventional modes of behaviour, is put in the female role of caring for the child. He is seen doing so in the narrative, for the child is not simply consigned to conventional absence, invisible in the care of servants. This change of role has actually been forced on Mengen by Faustine, despite the fact that she could not change his attitude to her. By these two adjustments of conventional gender roles  Hahn-Hahn has intimated the potential for change, the possibility of overcoming the polarised perceptions of society. Within this novel there is the germ of change in terms of the authoress' rejection of a purely stratified gender-specific representation of individual and social psychology.

It is of course only one example of the realist fiction being written by women at this period, that is before major male figures came to dominate the German realist canon. It was a period which saw the replacement of the idealised heroine by more realistically portrayed women, whether in more tendentious novels such as Fanny Lewald's *Jenny* (1843) in which the equally beautiful, talented, intelligent heroine is denied happiness and fulfilment by anti-Semitic prejudice in German society, or in Johannah Kinkel's account of a family woman's fate living in exile in *Hans Ibeles in London* (1860). Hahn-Hahn's refreshing scepticism,[27] her literary sophistication - call it stew if you like - her ear for dialogue and eye for body language combined with a capacity for analysing human behaviour and recognising socially conditioned patterns of manipulation make this novel worthy of a place in the canon of nineteenth-century realist literature.

---

[27] See A. Schweitzer and S. Sitte, 'Tugend - Opfer - Rebellion. Zum Bild der Frau im weiblichen Erziehungs- und Bildungsroman' in *Frauen Literatur Geschichte. Schreibende Frauen vom Mittelalter bis zur Gegenwart*, ed. H. Gnüg and R. Möhrmann, (Stuttgart, 1985), p.165.

# Auerbach's *Schwarzwälder Dorfgeschichten* and the Quest for 'German Realism' in the 1840s

by Edward McInnes

The publication of the first volume of Auerbach's *Schwarzwälder Dorfgeschichten*, Prutz declared in 1859, was an event of outstanding importance in the literary history of the previous decade. No other work in these years, he claimed, had had such an uplifting, unifying impact, had managed to inspire both critics and ordinary readers with such an exhilarating sense of discovery.[1]

Prutz is not overstating the case here. The appearance of the seemingly modest volume in 1843 (followed some five years later by a second collection) galvanised the general reading public and released in the critical establishment a degree of excitement, of jubilation even, which literary historians have always found hard to explain. Auerbach's work succeeded in winning extravagant approval from commentators normally guarded in their judgements and in drawing together critics who had agreed to differ on almost everything else.

I think that it is well worth looking more closely at these earliest reviews and critical discussions of the *Schwarzwälder Dorfgeschichten*. To get any further, however, we have to try to see them in the context of the literary-theoretical

---

[1] R. Prutz, *Die deutsche Literatur der Gegenwart*, (Leipzig, 1850), Bd. II, 233f..

discussions of the early 1840s, and in particular of the attempt of critics at this time to explore the possibilities of a vital realistic social novel in Germany.

Throughout the late 1830s commentators had lamented with deepening disquiet, the artistic weakness of the German novel and repeatedly pointed out its failure to match the robust achievements of the novel in France and Britain. While writers in these countries had succeeded in making the genre a powerful organ of contemporary experience, German novelists (they declared) were still strangely ill at ease with the realities of social existence and uncertain in their attempt to articulate the concerns and hopes of ordinary people.[2] Seldom was this incessant complaint expressed more sharply than in the anonymous review of Carleton's *Sketches* in *Blätter für Literatur und bildende Kunst* in 1837:

> Recht viel Innerlichkeit, Gemütlichkeit, Betrachtung und Divination finden wir in unserm Romane, aber das praktische Leben mit allen seinen gegenwärtigen Interessen suchen wir vergebens; Theorien, Spekulationen und Ideen aller Art haben wir die Menge, aber ein Bild unseres eigenen Seins und Treibens finden wir nirgends ... Im englischen Romane, in allen schriftstellerischen Produktionen finden wir gerade das Entgegengesetzte in Ziel und Richtung; der Geist der Volkstümlichkeit durchweht sie wie ein kräftiger Lebenshauch, die Interessen der Gegenwart sind allenthalben vertreten, das freie Wort bemächtigt sich aller Richtungen des sozialen Lebens.[3]

There was, however, something fundamentally disingenuous about the readiness of commentators at this time to denigrate the German novel by comparing it with the more compelling, socially immediate works appearing in France and England. For as most of them were very soon forced to admit there was no valid critical basis for such comparisons. Indeed those who most enjoyed making them were often the keenest to admit that the position of the German novelist as observer and analyst of society was much more restrictive and infinitely less rewarding than that of his counterparts in the great metropolitan countries.[4] The novelist in Germany, as reviewers and critics were constantly pointing out, was trapped in a broken, retarded society which was inescapably petty and colourless in its everyday concerns and aspirations. Almost every

---

[2] For a fuller discussion of this tendency see H. Steinecke, *Romantheorie und Romankritik*, (Stuttgart, 1975), Bd. I, 153ff. See also E. McInnes, "Innerlichkeit, Alltag und Gesellschaft' in *Die fürstliche Bibliothek Corvey*, ed. R. Schwörling and H. Steinecke, (Munich, 1992), pp.193 - 204.

[3] *Blätter für Literatur und bildende Kunst*, 1837, p. 262.

[4] Steinecke, *Romantheorie*, op. cit., 155f.

discussion of Dickens' early novels in the late 1830s, for instance, emphasised the fact that they were essentially London novels, that they grew out of the novelist's vision of the mighty Capital as an arena which embraced all the shaping energies, political, cultural and artistic, of English national life.[5] In London, as commentators tirelessly declared, Dickens *saw* the life of Britain; in the events taking place around him he could grasp the substantial existence of the whole kingdom at this moment in its great historical destiny.

The provincial German novelist, by contrast, was denied such immediate, inspiring access to the collective experience of his fellow countrymen. Lacking 'jede großartige Öffentlichkeit' (in Prutz' phrase), he was driven to observe the life of the nation in the parochial world of the *Provinzstadt* or *Residenz*, a setting itself ironically expressive of disjunction, smallness and historical failure. How - critics rhetorically enquired - could a literary work of national range and power come into being in a society so fragmented, inconsequential and so at odds with its people's longing for unity?

The tendency of critics to decry the German novel by comparison with developments abroad was also equivocal in another fundamental respect. Despite their ready admiration for the realistic social novel in France and England the overwhelming majority of commentators were concerned to emphasise the distinctiveness of the German novel tradition and to assert its relevance to the contemporary world. The national novel for which they longed - they constantly insisted - must develop out of the experience of the German people and embrace the idealistic impulses which informed the conception of the classical German novel.

Despite the readiness of critics to make such dogmatic statements of general objectives they were noticeably very reluctant to engage in practical considerations of the enormous problems facing the German writer who attempted to renew the conception of the *Bildungsroman* in an age which, as they acknowledged was increasingly sceptical in its outlook. In this respect the discussions of Immermann's *Die Epigonen* (1836), which was generally regarded as the most significant German novel of the mid 1830s, mark an important shift in the literary critical reflections of the time. The appearance of this very ambitious, very German novel brought considerations of the genre down to earth with a bump. It forced critics to consider in a much more concrete, pragmatic way a whole range

---

5 See E. McInnes, '*Eine untergeordnete Meisterschaft?*' *The Critical Reception of Dickens in Germany 1837-1870*, (Frankfurt am Main, 1991), pp.45ff.

of questions which had generally been discussed in abstract speculative terms.

Many critics were ready to acknowledge that in *Die Epigonen* Immermann was attempting to realise a form of novel which corresponded closely to their theoretical demands: a novel which was broad in its social concerns, challengingly modern, yet firmly rooted in the classical German tradition. [6] The author, as Laube for example pointed out, made it quite clear that he was following in Goethe's footsteps and attempting nothing less than to write 'den Wilhelm Meister der modernen Verhältnisse'.[7] Most commentators were in fact impressed by the contemporaneity of the work and applauded Immermann's energetic imaginative drive to depict all the disparate aspects of contemporary social existence and show his hero, Hermann, as caught up in a complex world in process of rampant, disconcerting change.

Despite all such positive initial acknowledgement, however, the responses of contemporary critics to *Die Epigonen* were profoundly ambivalent. Although Immermann had significantly extended the social range of the German novel, he had failed, most commentators believed, to bring about the final imaginative resolution which was his artistic goal. In fact, in the view of many it was precisely the force of his pessimistic social vision which had undermined his attempts to realise the moral development of Hermann as a powerful, compelling inner process: the novelist's view of his hero as a being engulfed in a disjointed impenetrable world had overwhelmed his capacity to realise Hermann as a significant moral protagonist.

Here, as Mundt emphasised, the discrepancy with *Wilhelm Meisters Lehrjahre* was unmistakable:

> Während Wilhelm Meister alle Weltobjekte in seine Persönlichkeit verarbeitet ... , findet sich bei Hermann ein Zwiespalt, der an einem gewissen coquettierenden Bewußtsein der Zerrissenheit festhält.[8]

Kühne also stressed what he saw as the basic incoherence in the conception of Immermann's novel. Hermann, he argued, far from attempting to come to terms with the society in which he lives, is intent simply on escaping from it. He uses the privileges of his wealth and the freedom it gives him to retreat to 'ein grünes

---

[6] For a detailed discussion of this see E. McInnes, 'Zwischen *Wilhelm Meister* und *Die Ritter vom Geist*', *DVjs*, 43 (1969), 487 - 514.

[7] H. Laube, *Geschichte der deutschen Literatur*, (Stuttgart, 1840), Bd. IV, 17.

[8] Th. Mundt, *Geschichte der Literatur der Gegenwart*, (Berlin, 1842), p. 589.

Plätzchen', a backward, rustic haven, as yet untouched by the ravaging processes of technological development which terrify and appal him.[9] Kühne, like Mundt and many other commentators, regarded the ending of the novel as evasive, and as evidence of Immermann's failure to reconcile the split between the inward self and the actual world of society which was the essential aesthetic function of the *Bildungsroman*. In *Die Epigonen*, they claimed, the analysis of social conditions ran parallel to the presentation of the hero's inner development, but these two basic impulses of the novelist's concern did not really impinge on and modify one another. Immermann, they concluded, had failed to achieve the embracing, reconciliatory vision to which he aspired.[10]

The intense critical controversy surrounding *Die Epigonen* in the late 1830s had a deep and, I think, lasting impact on underlying critical attitudes to the German novel. Looking back we can see that it had the effect of dampening expectations and intensifying the general despondency about the state of the genre in Germany. Literary theorists and critics did, it is true, continue to insist that a truly contemporary, socially responsive German novel must embrace the idealistic energies of the classical German tradition. They seemed now, however, much more fully aware of the intractable difficulties facing the novelist who sought to achieve this renewing synthesis. The dawning recognition of critics in the early 1840s that Immermann's ambitious experiment had failed to inspire any serious successor served only further to enforce the sense that the novel in Germany was caught in an impasse.

We have to see the reception of the first volume of the *Schwarzwälder Dorfgeschichten* in the context of this deepening critical pessimism about the situation of the German novel. The intense excitement which Auerbach's work aroused among contemporary commentators stemmed, it seems, from their immediate intuitive recognition that it marked a crucial break-through, that it took the novel in Germany into a decisive new phase of its development. This assurance informs many of the most important early reviews in which critics were largely concerned to assess the character of the revolution in the novel which in their view Auerbach had brought about.

Almost all the contemporary critics who hailed the originality of the *Schwarzwälder Dorfgeschichten* emphasised the vivid evocative force of

---

9 F. Kühne, *Porträts und Silhouetten*, (Leipzig, 1843), Bd. II, 92.

10 See E. McInnes, 'Zwischen *Wilhelm Meister* und *Die Ritter vom Geist*', op. cit..

Auerbach's sharply detailed portrayal of peasant life and saw in this the realisation of a kind of social authenticity, of truth to everyday life, which was new in German literature.[11] Yet most of these critics were also at the same time concerned to stress the poetic, heightening tendency of Auerbach's realism and to claim that in his commitment to the parochial world of the Black Forest peasant he had created a vision of existence which had a powerful national significance. In penetrating the narrow realm of the rural village he had succeeded in laying bare areas of emotional and spiritual experience which German readers of all backgrounds could acknowledge as their own. In these stories, as Hermann Marggraff put it, Auerbach evoked 'die Kernpoesie des deutschen Gemüts'.[12]

Other commentators also emphasised the deeply affirmative, celebratory quality of Auerbach's presentation of rural life. In a much discussed article in 1843 J.E. Braun saw Auerbach, like his mentor Immermann, as making a powerful moral stand 'gegen die Lüge der modernen Gesellschaft, gegen ihre Hohlheit, Unwahrheit und Halbheit' by committing himself to the organic world of the peasant where 'die alte reine Sitte so ursprünglich und blühend erhalten hat'.[13] Karl Hagen, in very similar terms, saw Auerbach as concerned to reveal den guten Kern' which still survived intact in the rural population. He saw the Schwarzwälder Dorfgeschichten as the German counterpart to Sue's Mystères de Paris. Whereas the French novelist exposed the depravity and crime in the back-streets of the great city, Auerbach evoked a wholesome, uplifting world:

> Der deutsche Schriftsteller ... führt uns unmittelbar in die Mitte von Volkszuständen, wo noch die stille Natur waltet, wo das Heiligtum einer naturgemäßen Entwicklung noch nicht durch die Laster der großen Welt getrübt worden ist.[14]

Such statements are characteristic of many at this time. They show the tendency of critics to stress the empirical, circumstantiating impetus of Auerbach's realism while at the same time emphasising its 'poetic', visionary dimension. The thrust of his imagination, they repeatedly claimed, was not just to expose what

---

[11] There is a representative selection of early discussions of Schwarzwälder Dorfgeschichten in Realismus und Gründerzeit, ed. M. Bucher et al., (Stuttgart, 1975), II, 148ff.

[12] H. Marggraff, Blätter für literarische Unterhaltung, (1844), p. 941.

[13] J. E. Braun, 'Ein Phänomen in der neuesten Literatur', Europa, (1843), pp. 127 - 34.

[14] K. Hagen, Jahrbücher der Gegenwart, (1844), pp. 810 - 17.

was ugly and corrupt but to transcend this in a perception of what was ultimately good and creative.

In this above all Auerbach appeared to many contemporary critics a writer who was nurtured and inspired by the unique idealistic traditions of the German novel.

**\*\*\*\*\*\*\*\*\*\***

## II

Auerbach's own prefatory comments on *Schwarzwälder Dorfgeschichten* appear in comparison with the subsequent claims of some of his first critics, noticeably specific and down-to-earth. In a letter sent with the manuscript of the first volume to Cotta in September 1842 he was concerned above all to stress the seriousness of his interest in peasant life. He explained that he was engaged in writing a series of stories,

> die innerhalb derselben Regionen gehalten das ganze häusliche, religiöse, bürgerliche und politische Leben der Bauern in bestimmten Gestaltungen zur Anschauung bringen wollen. [15]

In a foreword which appeared as part of an open letter to J.E. Braun in *Europa* in the following year he again stressed the pragmatic, documentary character of his work. [16] The village which is the setting of these stories, he pointed out, is not an imaginary one, or even a conflation of features taken from several real villages, but an actual location, Nordstetten, the place where he himself was born and grew up.

It is this village which he is depicting in close detail, from, as he says, the first house to the last. He is depicting the way of life in this community, the traditions, customs and day-to-day activities of the villagers as he himself has experienced them and knows them to be.

Auerbach is claiming here that he is writing about Nordstetten from first-hand knowledge: that he is describing it, as it were, from the inside, and can thus

---

[15] Quoted in A. Bettelheim, *Berthold Auerbach*, (Stuttgart, 1907), pp. 128f.

[16] B. Auerbach, 'An J. E. Braun vom Verfasser der Schwarzwälder Dorfgeschichten', *Europa*, (1843), pp. 33 - 6.

guarantee the authenticity of his record. At the same time, however, Auerbach also makes it clear that he sees peasant life from a quite different point of view. He is also observing it - he claims - from the outside, from the position of one who has lived for almost two decades in a more sophisticated, cosmopolitan world of which most of the inhabitants of Nordstetten know very little. As an outsider in this sense he is attempting to see the life of the community in the context of the development of German society as a whole. This two-eyed way of seeing, this probing double vision, will enable him (Auerbach clearly believes) to produce the full, diverse and balanced picture of peasant existence which his contemporaries demand. While yielding to the emotional hold of his childhood world upon him, acknowledging his roots as a *Bauernkind*, he also strives for a dispassionate intellectual understanding of the social-historical situation of the Black Forest peasant, its besetting problems and its unrealised possibilities. [17]

These introductory comments of Auerbach's were clearly meant to help ease contemporary readers into the imaginative world of the *Schwarzwälder Dorf-geschichten*. In some respects, however, they may have raised false expectations. The author's concern to emphasise his serious, empirical interest in peasant life, his will to scrutinise it closely and in its every aspect, could well have created the impression that he was aiming at a kind of rigorous social realism which was in fact quite foreign to his intentions. This discrepancy between the apparent implications of his preface and his actual artistic preoccupations is most obviously apparent in one very fundamental area of his apprehension of peasant life: in the inconsistent and often seemingly casual way he portrays the general economic conditions governing the life of the village community. For a writer committed to a full systematic investigation of the day-to-day existence of the peasant Auerbach shows remarkably little interest in his actual working life. [18] He does not explore in any penetrating way the different kinds of work in which the inhabitants of Nordstetten spend most of their waking hours, nor does he attempt to show how the labours of these different individuals interlock in the collective economy of the

---

[17] There has been a noticeable revival of critical interest in Auerbach's work in the last twenty years or so. I have received help and stimulus particularly from the following: W. Hahl, *Reflexion und Erzählung*, (Stuttgart, 1971); P. Zimmermann, *Der Bauernroman*, (Stuttgart, 1975); J. Hein, *Dorfgeschichte*, (Stuttgart, 1976); U. Baur, *Dorfgeschichte*, (Munich, 1978).

[18] References to *Schwarzwälder Dorfgeschichten* are to Berthold Auerbach, *Gesammelte Schriften*, Bd.1-20, (Stuttgart, 1857f.). *Der Tolpatsch, Befehlerles* and *Ivo, der Hajrle* are in Vol.1; *Florian und Creszenz* and *Der Lautenbacher* are in Vol.2; *Sträflinge* and *Die Frau Professorin* are in Vol.3; *Lucifer* is in Vol.4.

village. Just as surprising is the fact that Auerbach makes so little effort to lay bare the peculiar psychological pressures inherent in the grinding struggle for economic survival which dominate the lives of the vast majority of the rural population. Auerbach does certainly acknowledge at times the peculiar precariousness of a way of life which is inescapably dependent on the vagaries of wind and weather. The opening section of *Lucifer* (1847), for instance, gives a horrifying picture of the timeless vulnerability of the peasant to incalculable natural disaster (pp. 9 ff.). But neither here nor elsewhere does Auerbach present this vulnerability as the controlling condition of peasant life, much less make clear the extent to which it entails for countless families a life lived under the constant threat of financial ruin and, its consequence, famine. Auerbach, in fact, shows remarkably little concern to explore the degree of destitution in the rural population. When he does present cases of extreme poverty he is generally out to show that it is *not* the inevitable consequence of general economic-social circumstances. The extreme poverty of figures like Nazi in *Ivo, der Hajrle* (1843), Florian in *Florian und Creszenz* or Jakob in *Sträflinge* (1845), as the author makes quite clear, is self-inflicted.[19] It arises directly out of a moral failure for which they as individuals are responsible and which, he implies, is avoidable.

This is, I think, symptomatic of the basic thrust of Auerbach's presentation of the peasant figures in *Schwarzwälder Dorfgeschichten*. Though he speaks in his prefatory comments of observing the peasant within the context of the particular conditions of their rural environment, Auerbach's impelling moral concern is to show his protagonists as subjects, as beings capable of understanding, of choice and inner development. The most striking peasant figures in these early stories are individuals who by birth and upbringing are part of the village world but who are set apart from their fellows by powerful inner qualities of will, intellect or moral striving. Auerbach presents these figures - figures like Aloys, Ivo, Luzian, Jakob

---

[19] *Ivo, der Hajrle*, pp. 362ff.; *Sträflinge*, pp. 65ff.; *Florian und Creszenz*, pp. 34, 39. Of the misfortunes of the hero the author says in express judgement: 'Die Welt hat ihm nichts getan, er ist selber schuld an seinem Unglück' (p. 55). In *Die Frau Professorin*, however, there is a very disturbing incident which is unusual in the *Schwarzwälder Dorfgeschichten*. Reihenmaier, the visiting librarian, meets by chance an old man who tells him that he is on the verge of starvation. The latter informs him that he has been offered food by the village authorities but has felt obliged to turn it down because he has seven grandchildren all equally close to starvation, and he feels unable to eat in front of them (pp. 152f.). Auerbach does not pursue the causes of such impoverishment here but exploits the situation for a narrowly political purpose by showing how Reihenmaier's humanitarian interest in the situation leads to his blacklisting as an agitator in the *Residenz* and the eventual destruction of his career (p. 163).

and Lorle - as individuals who intuitively acknowledge their rootedness in the
sphere into which they are born, yet who are driven in their different ways by a
need to probe some deeper level of self, to engage a darkly felt sense of their
fuller human potentiality. Auerbach seems to see the drive of these figures to self-
recognition and fulfilment as something inherently spiritual which flows from the
deepest core of their personhood, and thus underlies the contingent pressures of
social experience.

It is perhaps in *Ivo, der Hajrle*, the most substantial story in the first volume
of *Schwarzwälder Dorfgeschichten* that Auerbach articulates in the most openly
polemic form this view of the peasant as developing moral protagonist. The titular
hero of the story is a sensitive, intellectually gifted peasant boy who from his
earliest years is impelled by the certainty that he is called to the priesthood. This
certainty, however, as Auerbach makes clear, is both complex and ambiguous. He
shows that Ivo's deeply contemplative nature has been shaped from infancy not
just by the conventional piety of the village community but also at a more
profound emotional level by the tense, fervent spirituality of his mother (pp. 216,
417). These influences, it soon becomes apparent, are also equivocally bound up
with the boy's naive materialistic longing for the status, power and easy
prosperity which he sees as the necessary endowments of the priesthood (pp.
215f.).

Despite these tensions in his self-awareness Ivo's belief in his sacred vocation
carries him through childhood and early adolescence. It is only when he enters the
seminary that he is assailed by the first crisis of doubt. Far from experiencing the
heightened spiritual fulfilment he had expected he finds the Church's demand for
the total obedience of mind and body as a disabling force of oppression which
negates his sense of identity:

> Er gehörte nicht mehr sich selber, er gehörte unaufhörlich einer
> Genossenschaft an ... . So kam sich Ivo in den ersten Tagen wie verkauft
> vor, denn nirgends war mehr freier Wille, alles Verordnung und Gebot;
> eine grausame Erfahrung stand vor seiner Seele: die Unerbittlichkeit des
> Gesetzes (p. 298).

In this state of deepening anguish Ivo receives a powerful moral summons
from an unexpected source. He is asked to read a letter from Aloys who as a
young man was driven by an overwhelming experience of failure to leave
Nordstetten and make a new life for himself in America. Ivo is immediately
impressed by the powerful sense of confidence and achievement which pervades

the letter (pp. 319ff.). Aloys reports that he and his fellow emigrés have founded their own village which they have called Nordstetten in homage to the place of their birth. This, however, he makes clear, is a reborn, progressive Nordstetten which the settlers have created in accordance with their vision of a free and just community. The inhabitants of the new Nordstetten are all conscious of their new found independence and of their essential equality with one another. They also acknowledge their shared responsibility for all communal affairs through their participation in the *Volksversammlung* from which no villager is excluded and in which each has equal status. They are even responsible Aloys points out, for the election of their own priest and of those who will serve as officers in their militia (pp. 322, 326f.).

This account of the new democratic order in New Nordstetten drives Ivo at once to reflect on the degree of oppression which is part of everyday life in contemporary German society in which the citizen has no defence against the arbitrary intrusions of state-power. But this letter has for Ivo a much more far-reaching and reverberative meaning. It releases the recognition of the power of ordinary human beings to create a social order which is at one with their deepest moral longings: an order in which the individual in the dignity of his freedom strives for his own fulfilment and so contributes to the full extent of his capacities for the good of all.

The story of Aloys has a profound and lasting moral impact on Ivo. The determination of the emigré to take charge of his existence, to begin life anew and in so doing to help bring into being a community which is democratic and humane, this foreshadows his own ultimate resolve to free himself from the morally deadening subjection to the authority of the Church in which he has been languishing. On leaving the monastery he is 'as if born again'. He marries his childhood friend, Emmerenz, and devotes himself to a life of hard, practical work in a saw-mill. In this new life, as Ivo himself makes clear, he seeks not just his own inner fulfilment but strives to commit all his talents to the welfare of his fellow men (pp. 465f.).

Auerbach is concerned to present the hero's re-affirmation of his ancestral world as a mature responsible act. Ivo embraces the life of the peasant with a renewed awareness of its values and possibilities and with the confidence of a man who has achieved self-knowledge through a long, lonely search for truth. *Ivo, der Hajrle* is, I think, both the most fundamental and openly programmatic of the early *Dorfgeschichten*. Auerbach asserts here in an overt and quite uncompromising way the individualism at the heart of his liberal philosophy and the intense moral and historical optimism which underlie it.

I would like now to turn briefly to two other early stories, *Befehlerles* (1842) and *Der Lautenbacher* (1843) which, albeit from a narrower and more specific point of view, deal with the crucial problem of growth, personal and communal, in the peasant world.

In *Befehlerles* Auerbach depicts the severe communal crisis which is brought about by the decision of the *Oberamtmann*, Relling, to repeal the traditional right of the married men of Nordstetten to carry a hand-axe on their persons (pp. 170ff.). This decision bewilders and enrages the whole male population of the village. Though all the men are gripped as one by a common sense of outrage, it is only through the leadership of one individual, the powerful imposing Buchmaier, that they are able (as Auerbach makes very clear) to express their anger as a group and direct it into effective action. Buchmaier is one of the villagers, but as he unquestioningly takes responsibility upon himself he seems constantly to grow in stature and to achieve unquestioned authority over his fellows (pp. 173f.). He alone seems able to grasp fully the nature of the anger which possesses the men of Nordstetten. He can see that for them the carrying of an axe is not simply a matter of practical utility but rather a right handed down by countless generations of Black Forest peasants and which thus represents a sacred trust they feel obliged to protect. It is also, Buchmaier senses, a custom which enshrines in a very special way the norms of independence, resolution and tenacity which are at the heart of their understanding of themselves and their position in society.

In one other crucial respect Buchmaier also shows controlling powers of leadership. He alone is able to recognise clearly that the protest of the villagers can be effective at the very highest level, since they act as men well known for their loyalty to the King and their respect for the rule of law (pp. 177f.). It is above all his power to communicate this assurance to the villagers that enables Buchmaier to channel their protest as a disciplined and dignified ritual of civic defiance without disorder or violence (p. 173).

The figure of Buchmaier dominates *Befehlerles*. He appears as a man thrust by the unexpected crisis in the community into a position of responsibility which calls forth his own latent powers of leadership and heightens the villagers' belief in themselves and their capacity for effective corporate action. As the example of Aloys serves to impel the inner development of Ivo, so the self-certainty of

Buchmaier helps to release powers of will and decision in the men of Nordstetten and thus to heighten their awareness of themselves as responsible citizens. The collective protest of the villagers in *Befehlerles* does in the end prove successful (p. 183). Relling, after a discrete lapse of time, is removed from office and, more significantly, Buchmaier is appointed *Schultheiß*. This is clearly an event of great psychological importance to the villagers, symbolising as it does a step forward in their persisting struggle to gain control over their own communal affairs.

*Der Lautenbacher* is also a parable of renewal and inner growth and appears in some respects as a logical sequel to *Befehlerles*.[20] In this affectionately ironic, deeply optimistic work Auerbach explores the function of education in the intellectual, moral and cultural development of the peasant community.

Adolf Lederer, the eponymous hero of the story is an ardent, young, seminary-trained teacher who comes to the village with little knowledge and no direct experience of peasant life. He is driven by a strong, idealistic desire to educate the local people, to help them achieve a liberating understanding of their existence. His pedagogic aims are determined - as Auerbach makes clear - by a preconceived view of the peasant as a retarded, spiritually constricted being, · imprisoned animal-like in a material world which precludes self-awareness and transcending vision (pp. 106f., 144).

Lederer's day-to-day involvement in the life of the village forces him, however, to modify more and more deeply these preconceptions. Through his close contacts with different members of the local community and above all through his growing love for Hedwig, an uneducated peasant girl, the teacher comes to see the futility of his unthinking attempt to force on the villagers his own fixed, academic notions of *Bildung*. His aim, he now recognises, should rather be to foster those profound energies of feeling and imagination inherent in the consciousness of the peasant population which are enshrined in countless local traditions of song and legend (pp. 192f.). The cultural development of the peasants, Lederer now sees, must grow out of their own distinctive spiritual and cultural heritage, and be shaped by their own deepest yearnings. He makes great practical efforts to fulfil this new sense of pedagogic purpose. He throws himself into the study of the dialect of the area and learns to love its rough, pungent beauty (p. 205). He explores the treasury of local folk-song and traditional

---

20 A number of the villagers who appeared in *Befehlerles* reappear in *Der Lautenbacher*, including Buchmaier in his new position as *Schultheiß*.

sayings, and studies the work of Sebastian Sailer, an Upper-Swabian folk-poet, with a view to using it as a basis for productive language teaching in the classroom. Outside school hours Lederer makes more and more fruitful encounters with the progressive enquiring members of the village community (pp. 217ff.). He discusses topical newspaper articles with them, founds a choral society and a club in which they can explore literary works previously inaccessible to them. Here, as in all other areas of contact with the villagers, the force and independence of their responses repeatedly surprise him. In his attempts to educate his 'pupils', Lederer is aware that he too is being educated, that he is still in the process of becoming the teacher which the peasants need.

In the three stories we have been discussing, as also in others like *Der Tolpatsch*, *Lucifer* and *Die Frau Professorin*, Auerbach is exploring a crucial development in the peasant's understanding of himself. The author is preoccupied here with protagonists who, as we have seen, are in one way or another exceptional in the context of the village community. Auerbach's aim, however, is to show that they are exceptional only in the degree to which they exhibit capacities of mind and spirit which are characteristic of the peasant population as a whole. In this sense he is presenting these protagonists overtly as representative figures who show the power of the peasant for inner regeneration, his ability to grow in response to the accelerating momentum of historical developments. These stories trace the process through which the peasant characters break through to a new consciousness of their individual and communal responsibilities and thus to a liberating recognition of their potentiality as moral agents. In the context of Auerbach's conception they all appear (to use Reihenmaier's description of the sceptical inn-keeper in *Die Frau Professorin*) as 'Bürger der Zukunft', both agents of change in the contemporary world and portents of the new open, unified society which is coming into being.

It is not surprising that critics in the 1840s saw in this positive, uplifting vision a far-reaching attempt on the part of Auerbach to renew the idealistic conceptions of the classical German novel by assimilating them to contemporary tendencies of thought and awareness. His work, they repeatedly claimed, was impelled by a perception of organic unfolding, of self-realisation from within, which underlay the conception of the Goethean *Bildungsroman*; here, however, the essential protagonist was no longer the single, inward individual but an entire social group which moved inexorably forward towards the fulfilment of its historical destiny. Auerbach's achievement as a contemporary writer lay for these critics in the fact that he had succeeded in realising his idealistic perception in the terms of a probing, pragmatic realism, which gained the intellectual and imaginative consent of the contemporary reader.

The enthusiasm with which so many early reviewers greeted the *Schwarzwälder Dorfgeschichten* shows that in these pre-revolutionary years, the historical optimism informing the conception of these stories did not appear as speculative or fanciful, but as grounded in, and sustained by, actual social experience. It is quite remarkable looking back how few commentators fundamentally questioned Auerbach's presentation of many of his rural figures as such intensely reflective, questing individuals able to express complex ideas in literate, discriminated German, even though this was at odds with their view of the essentially realistic character of his work. His positive, elevating view of the peasant found eager acceptance both in the critical establishment and in the general reading public, and was obviously one of the main reasons for the great popularity of the *Schwarzwälder Dorfgeschichten* at this time. Readers of all kinds - the overwhelming majority of whom were middle-class - found this view moving and, we can assume, reassuring, demonstrating as it did the wide communality of moral attitudes and interests underlying the divisions in contemporary society. Auerbach's apprehension of the peasants as men and women who instinctively embrace the values of independence, diligence and personal and civic responsibility succeeded to a very large degree, it seems, in evoking a sense of national cohesion and confidence throughout the German states.

**********

III

This brings us face to face with the problem of assessing the position of the *Schwarzwälder Dorfgeschichten* in the literary developments of the 1840s. We have, as I see it, to ask ourselves one fundamental question: to what extent did these works represent - as many contemporary critics believed - the achievement of a distinctively German form of realism - a realism which fused the ideal values of the German literary tradition with the empirical awareness and social concern of the mid-nineteenth century?

Auerbach's aim, as we have seen, was to record the life of the peasant community in Nordstetten in close authentic detail while at the same time seeking to set it in the context of contemporary social developments in Germany. It seems to me, however, that his attempts to fulfil this aim were restricted by the pressures of his liberal ideology to a degree which he himself, could not fully recognise; that his compelling sense of political purpose constantly subverted his quest for social realism.

His attempts to define the crucial rôle of the peasantry in the political movements of the time forced him to disregard the vast sections of the rural population which were entrapped in severe poverty and destitution, and to place in the centre of attention characters who are able, both materially and intellectually, to transcend the conditions governing the lives of the majority of the peasants. But precisely these capacities which make these figures amenable to Auerbach's political purpose release them from the fundamental predicaments of their fellow villagers. Those factors which distinguish them as 'Bürger der Zukunft' undermine their standing as representatives of the general peasant population.

When we look at these two first volumes of *Schwarzwälder Dorfgeschichten* from this point of view Auerbach does seem open to the charge first made by his friend Moses Hess in 1845 that he had betrayed the peasants by failing to expose the severe poverty ravaging their communities. Hess complained in a letter to Auerbach that far from showing his readers the awful truth, he had written sentimental fables which allowed them to turn their backs on the peasants in the false assurance that nothing was seriously amiss. Such criticism cannot have come as a surprise to Auerbach. In his article in *Europa* in 1843 he had attempted to preempt it by insisting that his function as a creative artist was quite distinct from that of a social propagandist and that his work could only lead indirectly (and thus belatedly) to reforms in the conditions of the rural population. Such a disclaimer, however, does not meet the more fundamental criticism of Auerbach's 'realism' which is, I think, implicit in Hess' criticism: the rejection of Auerbach's claim that he is giving an accurate and comprehensive account of peasant life. His failure to record the full severity of the poverty affecting the rural communities did not just represent (as Hess suggests) a neglect of his basic humanitarian duty but an *artistic* failure: his evasion as a novelist of the situation of the peasants in its actuality and thus of its far-reaching implications for German society as a whole. For it was poverty above all which was eroding the age-old structures of peasant life in the 1840s. Under its deepening impact agricultural workers were already forsaking their communities in ever greater numbers and moving to the great industrial centres where they were being absorbed into a vast anonymous urban proletariat. This was a process which Auerbach did recognise and deeply lamented. As a social novelist, however, he was unwilling or unable to acknowledge its determining historical significance and to explore its economic-social causes. This failure to confront directly the cataclysmic upheaval engulfing the peasant world deprives his chronicle of contemporary rural life of vital historical relevance. Auerbach's overriding concern with the individual, his belief that the renewal of society could only arise out of the endeavours of single committed individuals working together, made it impossible for him to recognise the irresistible momentum of the economic forces undermining the village communities. It was not the political capacities of outstanding members of the peasantry which were shaping their future but the destitution and despair of their nameless, voiceless rural underclasses, classes almost completely absent from the social world of the *Schwarzwälder Dorfgeschichten*.

# Historical Realism

by Peter Skrine

It may be taken as almost axiomatic that realism is concerned with the present. The nineteenth-century realist author sets about creating a descriptive analysis of the contemporary world, of contemporary society, which readers will recognise and accept as their own. Realist works are set in more or less specific places, in what may loosely be called the present day. They narrate events which could plausibly have occurred during the lifetime of their authors and readers, the end of the story conventionally or apparently coinciding with the moment at which the book is being written and read. Great works of German nineteenth-century realism bear this out: *Zwischen Himmel und Erde, Die Frau Professorin, Geld und Geist, Soll und Haben, Kalkstein, Der grüne Heinrich.* Each of these is set in a specific though usually unspecified part of the German-speaking world, and always in what may be described as the present day; that is, they narrate events which are happening as we read, or a sequence of events which leads to the point at which we put the book down, the story told. Often, too, a realist work points ahead to the immediate future by suggesting potential shifts and changes of attitude and social behaviour which are likely or, perhaps, desirable. In so far as they describe events that are over and past, they do so on the tacit understanding that what has recently happened is an integral part of the process of history understood as progress.

If the axiom that realist writers are primarily concerned with the present day applies more or less generally to post-romantic realism, it is even truer of that earlier wave of pre-romantic realism that was responsible for the greatest feats of the eighteenth-century creative imagination. The novels of Fielding and Goldsmith, of Richardson, Fanny Burney, Prévost and Choderlos de Laclos, present contemporary characters and situations clearly set in the present, which is their sole concern. So, too, do their German counterparts, such as Goethe's *Werther* (1774) and Miller's *Siegwart* (1776), a fascinating but usually overlooked novel which gives a vivid account of life in provincial Germany and which ran it a close second, but whose subtitle 'Eine Klostergeschichte' encourages misapprehensions on the part of the badly-read literary historian. Indeed one might go so far as to argue not only that the mid-eighteenth century was the heyday of truly prosaic realism, but that its fiction exerted an influence on the realism of the mid-nineteenth century so profound and far-reaching that many a later author chose to set his own realistic narratives in it. Take for example Thackeray, whose most mature novels, *Henry Esmond* (1852) and *The Virginians* (1857 - 59), transport their readers back to the eighteenth century through their author's extraordinary empathy with it, an empathy generated and achieved by meticulous attention to social and linguistic detail, as well as to historical fact.

From the European point of view, however, it was of course the example set by Scott which proved decisive. As Scott worked his way back in time from the eighteenth century to more distant, 'romantic' periods, he not only demonstrated that realism could also be an effective way of approaching the past; in Germany's case he also filled a gap in the evolution of the novel, which, between the 1780s and the 1830s, had largely been sidetracked by the development of the *Entwicklungsroman* or *novel of identity*, and by the revival of romance by the writers of the Romantic Movement. It was not until the late 1820s that a genuine trend towards realism becomes discernible in German fiction, notably in the sequence of masterpieces written by Tieck during this phase of his long career (e.g. *Der Aufruhr in den Cevennen*, 1826; *Hexen-Sabbath*, 1831). The shape that trend was to take is significantly different from the norm in other European literatures - most obvious is the preference of major writers for shorter narrative forms - and in its shaping the challenge of the past and of how to handle it in realist terms was to play an essential part, though one that can often be overlooked by literary historians.

The purpose of what follows is to identify, describe and give examples of six different categories or types of historical realism in mid-nineteenth-century German narrative literature, proceeding from the least obtrusive type to the most daring and outspoken. These categories, and the works that are good examples of them, demonstrate that there is indeed a whole dimension of nineteenth-century realism that is not really concerned with the present, and which deserves to be called 'historical' in the sense that it is the medium for stories which are deliberately and clearly set in what we - like their original readers - recognise as specific periods in the past. This strand in nineteenth-century German realism includes a range of masterpieces which, though they are often little known, deserve recognition because they place the historical element so entirely at the centre of their realist narrative purpose that their aesthetic success and their effect on the reader depend directly on it.

## Type 1

This type follows directly on from what has just been said. It will not have escaped the notice of most readers that mid-nineteenth-century German works of fiction are often set in the previous century. Though there may be nothing to compare with Thackeray before the novels of Fontane, there are in fact many works which share this common characteristic. Take Storm, for instance. From early on in his career his best work is characterised by an acute sense of the passing of time and the transience of earthly things - a stoic, almost baroque mood that is both manifested in and counterbalanced by his compulsion to go back in time. Indeed it is this urge that stimulates his best narratives. His last work, *Der Schimmelreiter* (1888) emphasises this. But in fact it is a characteristic already vividly present in an early story of 1854: *Im Sonnenschein*. Its opening, an epitome of Stormian writing, is as vivid and immediate - that is, 'realistic' - as anything he wrote. Konstantin, a young officer, is waiting in the garden for Fränzchen to finish work and come down to join him. Absent-mindedly he doodles in the gravel with his cane as the sunshine pours through the leaves of a honeysuckle arbour and dapples the ground with light and shade; the palpable immediacy of the experience - the moment - is unforgettably crystallised. Having established this immediate sense of the experienced moment, - the narrative present - the story suddenly relegates it to a past that is beyond recall. The next paragraph begins 'Es war eine andere Zeit; wohl über sechzig Jahre später', the past tense of the verb 'sein' nevertheless placing past and present on an equal footing. An old grandmother is reminiscing about her Aunt Fränzchen and what became of her: the garden that was so real that day long ago exists no more, and in the family vault the old coffins are disintegrating. Yet, as Storm presents it, no mouldering coffin or other 'realistic' emblem of mortality can cancel out the vitality and validity of that day long past; in the story he tells, it is just as vivid and 'present' as the events of the story's other narrative present, sixty years later. *Im Sonnenschein* is poised between past and present. Death and life intermingle. Storm's later story, *Die Söhne des Senators* (1880) also opens with a coffin and a walled garden - powerful Stormian symbols - but it is different in technique, and belongs to a different category of historical realism, in that it takes place entirely in the good old days of the eighteenth century, when things in Husum were so different and, by implication, better.

Keller, too, is constantly being drawn back into the eighteenth century. Sometimes its living presence is still palpably there in works set in the contemporary world, such as the last Seldwyla story, *Das verlorene Lachen* (1874), in which the textile firm of the Glor family acts within the subtle narrative strategy of the text as a reminder of an older, more stable way of living and of doing business, and thus by implication as a scathing indictment of modern materialist short-term economic thinking. Sometimes, however, Keller applies his descriptive gifts to the portrayal of a past that predated him, but to which as a writer he was constantly drawn back. This occurs most memorably in his portrayal of Salomon Gessner in *Der Landvogt von Greifensee* (1878), a work set entirely in the eighteenth century. If in Storm's case the eighteenth century brings out the poignancy of time past or passing, and enhances the stark fact of mortality and oblivion, in Keller's it is an essential element in his ongoing analysis of the current state of human society and the human mentality as exemplified by the fictitious town of Seldwyla, about which as Stadtschreiber of Zurich he knew so much. It is no coincidence that the previous century plays such a major role in Keller's fiction; the ethos of the Zurich of his own day was still deeply rooted in the thinking and manners of the eighteenth century.

## Type 2

Let us now turn to another type of historical realism, the one best illustrated by the *Novellen* of Wilhelm Heinrich Riehl (1823 - 97) and the serious intentions underlying them. Riehl was a journalist and social historian whose essays were collected under the title *Naturgeschichte des Volkes als Grundlage einer deutschen Sozial-Politik* (1851 - 69), but who also wrote fiction that illustrates his views and findings. Here we have a very different approach to the whole question of the relationship between realism and history. To the modern reader the result may seem little more than *histoire romancée*; but Riehl claimed that his fiction was based on a sound factual grasp of period and historical process as well as on his insight into what makes a period tick. The preface to his *Kulturgeschichtliche Novellen* (Stuttgart and Augsburg: Cotta, 1856) states his position as follows:

> Der Dichter kann ein durchgebildetes Kunstwerk hinstellen, dem das kulturgeschichtliche Detail eine handgreifliche Lebensfrische gibt, deren das Drama entbehren muß; ein Kunstwerk, welches nicht bloß geschichtliche Zustände schildert, sondern in seinem Kern jenes höchsten sittlichen Inhaltes voll ist, der uns in jeglichem Menschengeschick die Hand des gerechten Gottes erkennen läßt. In solch echtem kulturgeschichtlichem Roman hat die Geschichte keine wächserne Nase und die Poesie behält doch Hand und Fuß. Ich lebe der Überzeugung, daß die Zukunft der modernen Epik in dem kulturgeschichtlichen Roman gegründet werden muß. ... Ein Kulturhistoriker hat diese Novellen geschrieben.

Here, then, it appears that fiction is to be based firmly on historical fact as interpreted by the social and cultural historian, who in this case is identical with the writer. Period detail matters because it reinforces truth to life and, in so doing, endows fiction with a high moral seriousness by laying bare the workings of Providence; genre-painting tends to take the place of evocative description, but as the backdrop comes into focus, the attention shifts from the great figures of history, whose deeds and passions are usually assumed to be the stuff of historical writing, and comes to rest on representative figures who for that very reason are fictitious if only in all but name. A Riehl story sets out to establish a specific period and place, and its fictitious events should possess a corresponding credibility, that is, they should be realistic. So, too, should its characters. And indeed this is usually the case.

Take for instance *Gräfin Ursula*, one of the 1856 'Kulturgeschichtliche

Novellen'. Less famous than *Der Stadtpfeifer* in the same collection (and yet another nineteenth-century evocation of the eighteenth century), it expands our purview by being set further back in time - in 1629, during the Thirty Years War. The countess who is its protagonist finds herself confronted with a moral dilemma characteristic of that period of denominational conflict, but which, in its actual detail, is specific to herself. The setting is 'real': Hadamar near Limburg in Hesse, and the story may well have been based on historical sources. But the characters Riehl develops are fictitious. He goes to considerable lengths to convey the feel of the period, though not, as one might expect, by extended and meticulous descriptions, so much as by occasional forays into a type of word-painting that suggests the syntax, rhythms and imagery of the German baroque without ever lapsing into pastiche. A good example occurs at the beginning of the last of the four chapters into which the *Novelle* is divided:

> Das Morgenrot ging in tiefem Purpur auf über den flachen Bergen des Elbgrundes. Die Gräfin saß im Erker und schaute in die rote Glut und wie im Traum rannen ihr die Farbentöne des unheimlich grell leuchtenden Himmels zu allerlei abenteuerlichen Bildern zusammen, daß sie sich die Augen rieb und sich fast schämte, kaum erst erwacht, schon wieder zu träumen. Das Sinnenspiel des Traumes verwandelte sich ihr dann in ein mystisches Sinnen und Weben, in ein träumendes Grübeln über die Dinge jener Welt, und oftmals blickte sie in den immer goldener glänzenden Lichtschein und sprach dabei vor sich hin Verse von dem himmlischen Morgenrot und dem Sonnenaufgang über den neuen Jerusalem, wie sie aus den mystischen Dichtern des ersten Jahrhunderts der protestantischen Kirche in Fülle ihr in den Sinn kamen. Schwachen Leibes, aber umso erregter im Gemüte - denn sie hoffte binnen Kurzem wieder Mutter zu werden - ergab sie sich neuerdings immer häufiger solch dämmerigem Dichten und Klingen der religiösen Phantasie.

Thus by alluding to German hymns and seventeenth-century mysticism, Riehl uses verbal, cultural and religious associations to create not just *Stimmung* but the lived reality of a past era.

## Type 3

The third type of historical realism is more familiar: indeed it is characterised by the use of a narrative device which became a stock feature of a certain type of nineteenth-century *Novelle*. Its favourite medium is that particular brand of

*Rahmengeschichte* in which a story set in the past is contained or encapsulated in a framework which is reassuringly located in the present. In a sense this type may be seen as a blend of the two already discussed and emphasises the importance placed by the historical realist writer on keeping at least the conclusion of his story in the here and now of the present - the present, that is, of his original readers. As a way of handling the past, it is a technique which lends itself to artificial narrative contortions, because it relies on chance encounters, or the discovery of ancient manuscripts whose survival into the present provides justification for the inset tale in the past. The form was widely used by German writers and was adopted with considerable success by Storm in the later years of his life. In *Zur Chronik von Grieshuus* (1884) the young narrator pieces together the history of a vanished manor house; *Aquis submersus* (1877) makes even bolder use of this narrative convention when the narrator finds himself inside the old house with the haunting inscription:

> Als ich sie [die kleine Lade] von dem Schranke, auf dem sie stand, herunternahm, fiel der Deckel zurück, und es zeigten sich mir als Inhalt einige stark vergilbte Papierblätter mit sehr alten Schriftzügen. 'Darf ich die Blätter lesen?' frug ich.
> 'Wenn's Ihnen Pläsier macht', erwiderte der Meister, 'so mögen Sie die ganze Sache mit nach Hause nehmen; es sind so alte Schriften; Wert steckt nicht darin.'

The master baker is of course mistaken, as we know. 'Ich aber las,' recalls the narrator, 'und hatte im Lesen bald alles um mich her vergessen.' Thus the spell is cast and reader, like narrator, finds himself translated back into a vanished past.


**Type 4**

This type of historical realism is more controversial. Its roots do not lie in the eighteenth century or the mid-nineteenth century's nostalgic idealisation of it, nor do they lie in any modern attempt to found fiction on fact or to present it as such. Rather it illustrates the survival, throughout the nineteenth century and its realism, of a strong romantic vein. Discussing Freytag's novel *Ingo und Ingraban*, the first of the *Bilder aus der deutschen Vergangenheit* (4 parts, 1859-67), in the *Augsburger Allgemeine Zeitung* in 1873, Berthold Auerbach, who had also begun his writing career as an historical novelist, observes:

Wir sind moderne Menschen mit realistischer Fassung des Lebens und der
Kunst; aber in den tieferen Gründen der Seele tönt noch ein
Waldhornklang und blüht noch eine blaue Blume der Romantik.

The remark is pertinent. We should bear in mind (but usually forget to do so) that
the expectations of the reader and lover of historical fiction were formed and have
always been decisively influenced by the continued availability of the classics of
the romantic period.These were often characterised by a vein of patriotism or
nationalism and an element of escapism and make-believe such as can be found in
the works of that much-enjoyed but now neglected writer, Fouqué: *Sintram*
(1815) is a good example. Such fiction delighted in transporting its readers back
into the 'days of yore' without all the 'realistic' ballast of historical accuracy
unless it was necessary to compensate for all-purpose modern stereotyped
characters and plot. One of the most influential historical novels of the German
nineteenth century had already established its popularity well before the rise of
realism in the 1840s. This was Hauff's *Lichtenstein* (1829), a work which may be
seen as standing on the threshold of German mid-nineteenth-century historical
fiction and at the parting of the ways as far as its subsequent development is
concerned. On the one hand it owes a good deal to romantic models and points
unambiguously forward towards historical romance - a type of popular literature
of which it may be seen as the classic prototype - yet many of its pages point
equally surely in the direction which Riehl was to develop in one way and Freytag
in another. But *Lichtenstein* was also the model for historical realist fiction of
another type. As far as popularity and originality went, this fourth type achieved
its most resounding success with *Ekkehard, eine Geschichte aus dem zehnten
Jahrhundert* (1855) by Viktor von Scheffel. Here the 'realistic' element is supplied
by a plot which the author drew from his own personal experience, but which he
projected back into the past; this historical dimension distanced the novel's
subjective element and was reinforced by the graphically portrayed tenth-century
setting in which that element is sublimated; indeed Scheffel's historical detail was
so thoroughly researched that the 'realism' of his novel might better be described
as historicism.

Appearing as it did right in the middle of the decade of Poetic Realism,
*Ekkehard* paradoxically acquired such status and popularity with German readers
that for a time it forced the earlier Romantic legacy of historical romance out of the
canon of 'good' literature and into the domain of children's literature and
*Trivialliteratur*. After all, historical romance lacks a serious scholarly tone and is

designed primarily to entertain, whereas Scheffel's stated objective is to achieve
'die geschichtliche Wiederbelebung der Vergangenheit' by means of 'eine
schöpferisch wiederherstellende Phantasie', as he observes in his preface.
Scheffel's conception of historical realism is in some ways akin to the sincere and
well-intentioned aims of the best Victorian architectural restorers. How different
his approach is from Freytag's exhaustive narrative survey of Germany's
evolution and from Riehl's well-meaning reconstructions of life in other periods,
both of which tend to give us everything except real life.


## Type 5

This fifth type was already welling up before Scheffel, Riehl, Storm and Keller
had begun to publish. It derives its energy from folklore and popular legend rather
than from nostalgia for the past or from the discoveries of modern historical
study. Like the category just mentioned, it may be said to have roots in
Romanticism. This time, however, it was the romanticism of the collectors of folk
and fairy tales, of local historians and antiquaries - a romanticism anticipated to
some extent by Kleist's *Michael Kohlhaas* and much closer to that of Scott than to
that of his German contemporaries, none of whom (with the exception of Achim
von Arnim) had Scott's ability to fuse it with the eighteenth-century realist
tradition. Type 5 had many manifestations but is particularly well illustrated by the
'other', lesser-known aspect of the creative achievement of one great writer,
namely Jeremias Gotthelf. Because he is so rightly lauded as a realist of the
present, Gotthelf's historical realism has too easily been overlooked. Yet a glance
at any of his so-called historical stories at once reveals that they share with the
better known realistic ones a deep rootedness in place and popular culture. How
does Gotthelf reconcile history and realism? Certainly not through the
proliferation of historical details, nor by writing in order to illustrate an underlying
concept of national history, or to indulge himself and his readers in escapism or
nostalgia for bygone times. The opening sentences of *Kurt von Koppingen* (1844;
revised version 1850) makes the essentials of his approach clear: it works in terms
that are imaginative rather than intellectual. The starting point of the story is the
authorial narrator's statement that human nature never changes: 'Die Gestalt der
Erde geht vorüber, gleich bleibt sich das Menschenherz für und für.' Yet we
should look at the past, he goes on, because it, too, has something of value to

show us:

> Nicht als Eintagsfliege ohne Zukunft hat Gott den Menschen geschaffen, und wer die ihm geordnete Zukunft genießen will, muß sich dazu stärken an der Vergangenheit. Wie jede Jahreszeit ihre Vorzüge hat und ihre Einflüsse, so jede Zeit im Weltenlauf.

Thus in Gotthelf's imaginative vision the past is counterbalanced by the future, with the implication that when we are immersed in a tale of long ago and are imaginatively and emotionally caught up by it, that future may well be our own present. For Gotthelf the past is by its very nature different from the present, yet the two are organically, even visibly linked: 'Vor sechshundert Jahren war es anders als jetzt im Schweizerlande', he writes 150 years ago, as his story of Kurt von Koppingen commences. It is a statement that remains perennially valid: things have always been different six hundred years ago. Moreover the story he is about to tell is situated in a location that still exists, and tangible vestiges of *then* may still be seen *now*:

> Im schönen weiten Aartale, nicht weit davon, wo es von der wilden Emme fast rechtwinklig durchschnitten wird, da wo jetzt das reiche Dorf Koppingen steht im Bernbiet, stand damals, wo jetzt noch auf dem Hügel, der Bühl genannt, Spuren zu sehen sind, ein kleines Schlößchen.

A similar approach may also be seen in *Die schwarze Spinne* (1842), where hearsay and a wooden mullion take the place of castle ruins. But this is not Gotthelf's only method. In *Der letzte Thorberger* (1843) he plunges his reader straight into the past at the deep end - not just into a period, but straight into the actuality of action and the reality of medieval life in all its starkness: 'Der Stoff ist tragisch und überreich,' he wrote, 'ich fürchte, er überwältige mich.'

This is how the story begins:

> Es war am heiligen Stephanstage im Jahre 1375, als eine riesige Schar in hartem Trabe einen steilen Hohlweg hinunterritt. Dicht und grau lag über Berg und Tal der Nebel, üppiger Reif bog die Bäume, schneidende Byse schüttelte denselben korbweise auf die Reitenden. Voran ritt in dunklem Harnisch ein hoher Ritter. Gewaltige Eile schien ihn zu jagen. Sein rotes Streitroß ließ er mächtig ausgreifen, sich des eisigen Weges nicht achtend, und, wenn hinter ihm Eisen klirrte, Reiter stürzten, er sah sich nicht um, er hemmte den Lauf nicht. Erst als er in einer Beugung des Weges ein niederes Tor aus dem Nebel sich hob ..., zügelte er rasch sein wildes Tier. Da der Weg steil abfiel bis an des Tores Rand, so stürzte mancher Ritter beim raschen Halt und mehr als einer glitt neben seinem Herrn vorbei hart

ans Tor und achtete sich des Torwächters nicht, der mit mächtiger Stimme die Reiter anrief, zu halten gebot und nach dem Namen fragte. 'Thorberg!' tönte es zum Turme hinauf; da fiel die Brücke, und durch das geöffnete Tor ritt Peter von Thorberg.

This is no projection back into the past: rather, it is an emanation or eruption of the past into the writing, and thus into the imaginations of readers of another, more sedate age.

## Type 6

The last type of historical realism to be considered follows on from the kind represented by Gotthelf, and the unique work which exemplifies it was in fact published in the same year as *Der letzte Thorberger*. *Maria Schweidler, die Bernsteinhexe* represents the most extreme form historical realism took in the nineteenth-century literature of Germany, or indeed of anywhere else. When it first appeared, without its author's knowledge, in 1843, on the instigation of Frederick William IV of Prussia, it was widely thought to be not a work of fiction at all but a genuine seventeenth-century document. The principal reason for this misapprehension is not far to seek. Wilhelm Meinhold's brutal tale of superstition and witchcraft is not just a compelling account of dire and sinister events on a Baltic island in the 1630s, it is one that is told without the least concession to contemporary taste. Not only is it uncompromising in its presentation; it is also written entirely in what purports to be, and sounds convincingly like, seventeenth-century German. It is the sort of story a seventeenth-century German might have written, if in those days they had written that sort of thing (which they didn't), and its meanderings awkwardnesses, especially before it gets going, can be put down to the 'fact' that its 'author' is an elderly pastor more used to writing rambling sermons than sustained narrative. By this strategy Meinhold safeguards his story's integrity and gives it an authenticity which convinces the reader despite himself, so entirely does the 'real' author disappear behind his fiction.

The notable thing about this darkest of mid-century German masterpieces is the way that the author manages to merge his own personality with the mind and mentality of his narrator, Pfarrer Abraham Schweidler, the incumbent of the parish of Coserow on the bleak Baltic island of Usedom. The tale Pfarrer Schweidler has to tell is full of circumstantial detail and personal concern, yet he has little or no inkling of what is going on in the life of his daughter, Maria, and is scarcely alive to the meaning of the events he is chronicling. The story is one of sex and witchcraft, but is conveyed by a man who knows little about such things, a technique which of course enhances the mystery of the strange goings-on he relates. Only very gradually, through his love for his daughter, does Pfarrer Schweidler come to some comprehension of the full horror of her denunciation and persecution as a witch, a narrative sequence culminating in his account of the day of her burning. Only her rescue in the nick of time by young Rüdiger may perhaps be seen as a concession to the taste of the 1840s, though it also happens to be exactly what might have happened in a seventeenth-century German novel.

To survey the subject of historical realism in mid-nineteenth-century German fiction from the vantage-point of Meinhold's masterpiece is to establish a criterion for historical realism that is so demanding that few other authors have accepted it and very few other works have ever lived up to it. *Die Bernsteinhexe* is indeed an almost faultless reproduction of the life of the past, as William Morris observed. Yet the authors operating in all the five other categories discussed here share with him the fundamental wish of all realist writers to merge their own identity and personality with that of the text, its narrator or main characters. Underlying this wish is the urge to achieve a sense of immediacy so great that in the act of reading the reader's imagination will spontaneously form its own direct relationship with a story it perceives to be true. If that story is set in the past, the challenge to the author's craft and to the reader's imagination is arguably all the greater. Hence the high regard in which historical fiction has been held, not least in the nineteenth-century Germany.

# Index of Names